The Ultimate Basic Training Guidebook

Tips, Tricks, and Tactics for
Surviving Boot Camp

The Ultimate Basic Training Guidebook

Tips, Tricks, and Tactics for Surviving Boot Camp

Sergeant Michael Volkin

SB

Savas Beatie

Cataloging-in-Publication Data is available from the Library of Congress.

First Savas Beatie edition 2005
Originally published in a private edition in 2004

ISBN 1-932714-11-1 (paper)
ISBN 1-932714-23-5 (hardcover)

SB

Published by
Savas Beatie LLC
521 Fifth Avenue, Suite 3400
New York, NY 10175
Phone: 610-853-9131

Savas Beatie titles are available at special discounts for bulk purchases in the United States by corporations, institutions, and other organizations. For more details, please contact Special Sales, P.O. Box 4527, El Dorado Hills, CA 95762, or you may e-mail us at sales@savasbeatie.com, or visit our website at www.savasbeatie.com for additional information.

Printed in the United States of America.

This book is dedicated to the men and women
of the United States military.

Thank you for your service and commitment to America.

Contents

Contents (continued)

Illustrations

Photos, charts, tables, and figures have been placed throughout this book for the convenience of the reader.

Foreword

by Major General
Robert J. Brandt, AUS

This guidebook, while simple in format, informs the reader about everything a recruit will need to know about basic training. Sergeant Volkin has reduced what is viewed by many as a complex military indoctrination process to a simple guide that will prepare a recruit for those essential items necessary to become a successful soldier.

Over my 45 years of military service, I managed to advance from Private E-1 to Major General. Some lessons I learned the hard way, and at other times, an entirely easier way. One thing I can tell you with conviction is that I was never presented with an impossible task. Military training is designed to move the individual one attainable step at a time. This allows the trainee to gain knowledge rapidly, giving him or her confidence to advance to the next, more complex, task.

Sergeant Volkin's emphasis on physical fitness is the first step to becoming a successful soldier. Physical fitness is the keel on which all your training begins. There is no easy way, and you must reach and maintain excellent physical conditioning. I strongly recommend that you take his advice and get a head start by working on your physical conditioning before you enter basic training. Physical fitness is a personal responsibility and it will remain so for the remainder of your military service.

Upon entering basic training, you will begin a socialization process where you will meet other trainees from throughout the United States. It is to your advantage to seek out those you know little about, whether from another region of this country, or a member of another race. There is a saying in the military that goes, "All blood is red," so becoming a soldier means you are all brothers in arms. There is simply no room for bigotry.

I would be remiss if I did not talk about having fun. Yes—fun. You can have fun and even enjoy many of the training events you will undergo. Over time, you will become proud of your individual and collective training achievements culminating with your graduation from basic training.

In summary, *The Ultimate Basic Training Guidebook* will put you on the right track to achieve success. Follow Sergeant Volkin's advice and you cannot go wrong.

Preface

I knew absolutely nothing about the military when I entered basic training. I had no military family history and no prior desire to ever join the military. It was on the tragic morning of September 11, 2001 that I realized what I was taking for granted all these years. Freedom, as wonderful as it is, is an uphill struggle, and comes with an enormous responsibility. It wasn't so much a decision, but a calling, that I joined the military - the Army Reserves.

I departed for basic training without an ounce of military knowledge one month after September 11, 2001. However, I used this lack of knowledge to my advantage. I took notes on everything, with the ambition that no recruit would have to go through basic training like I did, with no knowledge of what was in store for me. I listened to hundreds of soldiers share their advice, tips, and tricks on surviving basic training. When I was deployed shortly after basic training to serve in Operation Enduring/Iraqi Freedom, I had the time to organize the notes, add to them, and assemble the most practical basic training guide ever written.

This book is straightforward, short and easy to understand. Take advantage of the fitness routine in this book. Many hours of research and trial and error went toward creating the program. I believe there is no other fitness program that can get you in shape for basic training faster.

Bring this book with you to basic training. I hope you find this the most helpful book you have ever read.

Acknowledgments

There are many people to thank who have made this book possible. Special thanks go to Jerry Volkin, my publisher, Theodore P. "Ted" Savas, Sarah Stephan, Lee Merideth, Major General Brandt, Jon Allen, Yadhira Whittington, Joey VanBeek, Brian Vandenover, Misti Mokros, Kristina Gibbs, Ned Phillips and the many other soldiers who shared their advice, opinions, and good cheer.

The photos in this book were taken in Iraq during Operation Enduring /Iraqi Freedom. Photographs by Jon Allen, copyright 2004 (fenix207@hotmail.com).

Introduction

During World War I, President Woodrow Wilson's staff developed an eight-week course for military recruits. This course, known as basic combat training, taught new soldiers basic survival skills for combat situations. Today, after many decades of trial and error, a nine-week basic training course is used to physically challenge incoming recruits, test their mental toughness, and get them ready for military service in the finest army the world has ever known.

After your nine weeks of basic training, you will feel and act more confident about yourself than ever before. Basic training will test your capabilities and limits. Your leadership skills will develop. You will also be more marketable to future employers. Why? Because smart employers love to have people with a military background apply for job openings. They know what you have successfully accomplished. The environment you will endure at basic training is much more rigorous than any forty-hour workweek.

If I Had Only Known . . .

As I was passing through basic training, I realized there was so much I could have prepared for—*if I had only known*. When I completed basic training and began Army Reserve obligations, I discussed this topic with many other soldiers. To a person they agreed that preparing for basic training in advance of arrival was not only possible, but relatively easy to do—*provided a new recruit knew what to prepare for, and how to prepare for it.*

It is my hope that *The Ultimate Basic Training Guidebook* fills this need by teaching you what to expect, and how to avoid the most common problems experienced by new recruits. In a major way, this book follows the Six P's maxim: prior planning prevents piss poor performance. Avoiding problems keeps you out of trouble, and staying out of trouble will allow you to develop, thrive, and succeed during basic training.

This book will provide you with an invaluable training advantage and make your nine weeks of basic training more rewarding. However, it is not designed to teach you *everything* you need to know about basic training. There are two good reasons for this. First, if this book touched on everything from how to throw a hand grenade to how to operate a sincgar radio, you would be holding an 800-page instruction manual. Trying to read and memorize all those details would be both discouraging and counterproductive. Instead, *The Ultimate Basic Training Guidebook* allows you to focus on what is really important; the smaller details will be easy to learn once the main concepts are memorized. Second, it is impractical to learn how to assemble an M–16 rifle or fire a grenade launcher by reading an instruction manual. Such courses are best taught with hands-on training in the field.

"Why are you joining the military?" I am sure you have heard that question already; if not, you soon will. It is an important question to consider. Do you know the answer?

The military offers some fantastic incentives for joining, including a paid college education and even retirement pay (with twenty or more years of service). Many people join the military because of these incentives. Perhaps you are down on your luck and need a steady job, so your signed up for active duty; maybe you need some weekend work and signed up for the reserves. As good as these reasons seem, they will not be good enough.

Virtually anyone with prior or current military service will tell you that soldiers who joined because of the steady paycheck often end up unmotivated and frustrated. The greatest satisfaction you will receive from the military is knowing that you are a part of an elite fighting force. You will gain pride, confidence, and the admiration of most of your fellow American citizens. Hopefully, you joined (or are thinking of joining) because you want to serve your country in the greatest military on earth.

Many people enter the service with an inaccurate concept of what it means to be a soldier. Hollywood has embellished the soldier's image by creating movies with gruesome battle scenes. These types of movies sell tickets. No one is going to watch a movie about three soldiers experiencing kitchen duty.

The truth is that during your nine weeks of basic training you will learn how to kill enemy soldiers. That is every soldier's primary objective. However, think about what it takes to send one soldier to kill an enemy target. That soldier needs food, supplies, a vehicle (and someone who can fix it when it breaks), administrative support (such as the issuance of pay checks and insurance matters), clean water, medical support, and so on. Your job as a soldier is not to wake up in the morning, shoot the bad guys, and then climb back into your bunk for some shut-eye. You will perform a multitude of tasks, and few are as exciting as you see in the movies. The details of running an army, no matter how small they may seem, are an important part of the big picture.

So don't join the military because of the exciting fighting scenes you see coming out of Hollywood. Chances are, you could spend twenty years in the military and never fire your weapon at an enemy. On the other hand, you could be called to serve in a war right after you complete basic training. You won't know until it happens.

But rest assured, your nine weeks of basic training will prepare you for survival and integrate you into a team capable of awesome power. You don't need to kill people to serve your country. Remember that when your Drill Sergeant orders you to perform what seems to be worthless task. He knows what he is doing, and has your best interests at heart.

Good luck. You will need it. But you will need less of it if you carefully read this book and prepare yourself in advance.

Chapter 1

Drill Sergeants:
The Mental Game

"Keep your fears to yourself,
but share your courage with others."

—Robert Lewis Stevenson

Surviving basic training is much more a mental challenge than a physical one. This chapter will teach you how Drill Sergeants view recruits and what you can do to win their respect and the respect of your fellow recruits.

What to Expect

Drill Sergeants are among the finest soldiers in the military. Anyone who has been through basic training and served out their commitment to the United States military will tell you this. They receive extensive training to learn how to best to test your physical and mental toughness. Drill Sergeants can be both physically and mentally intimidating. It is good to know this going in, so you know what to expect and how to act (and interact) with them.

Drill Sergeants can be easily identified by their campaign hats. The hat to the left (Figure 1) is for male instructors; the hat below (Figure 2) is for female instructors.

Figure 1

Figure 2

For the first time in your life you will need to ask permission to go to the bathroom, to talk, to eat, etc. Your personality, as you know it, will be lost and you will be expected to think and act like everyone else. The logical question everyone asks is why does the military do this? This is not done to *scare* you. Rather, it is intended to *prepare* you. I cannot stress enough the importance of mental toughness. So swallow your pride and ego and pay close attention to the orders you receive.

> "A Drill Sergeant has one mission in life: to convert you from a civilian to a soldier."

Drill Sergeants have extensive experience dealing with recruits, and are trained to make your life as hellish as possible. Never (and I repeat) *never* say "Sorry, sir!" or "Thank you, sir! " to a Drill Sergeant. Ninety percent of what you should (and will) say is "Drill Sergeant, yes Drill Sergeant!" and "Drill Sergeant, no Drill Sergeant!"

Harsh criticism (i.e., calling you names, screaming, and so forth) is common for Drill Sergeants. They want to see if you can take a shot to your ego. The worst thing you can do mentally is to take criticism from a Drill Sergeant personally. Remember, it is never personal. Know all the while that they cannot physically harm you in any way.

The mission of a Drill Sergeant is to convert you from a civilian to a soldier. It is their job to break you down and build you up. You have joined the best military in the world. Your transition from civilian to soldier will be taught in a disciplined and rigorous manner. Superior training equals superior soldiers.

> **Did You Know?**
>
> Becoming a Drill Sergeant is not easy.
>
> Each Drill Sergeant who trains a recruit has already completed a stressful and rigorous course.

How to Gain Respect from Other Recruits and your Drill Sergeants

At the beginning of basic training, you will notice there are two types of recruits: the bosses and the workers.

The bosses are the "go get 'em," "gung-ho," "listen to what I say," recruits. The bosses love to shout orders at other recruits. They think they know what to do all the time—maybe because of their family has a proud military history, or because they had a friend who just finished basic training. Regardless of their reason for trying to act like a leader, most of them get themselves into trouble. The other recruits don't listen to them because they don't respect the bosses. Leaders are followed because they are respected (or in some cases feared). Drill Sergeants love to degrade and embarrass hotshot recruits.

The other type of recruit, the worker, is more passive than the boss. These recruits follow what anyone says. They appear to be intimidated by Drill Sergeants and they are easily persuaded. The workers will be the quiet type, waiting for someone, anyone, to tell

> **"Leaders are followed because they are respected."**

them what to do and where to be. These recruits often get into trouble because Drill Sergeants can smell fear. And guess what? Fear isn't allowed in the military—the U.S. military, anyway. So a Drill Sergeant thinks he must pay special attention to any recruit who displays even a whiff of fear.

I know what you are thinking. If a Drill Sergeant goes after bosses *and* workers, how can a recruit be successful at basic training without being a favorite target for Drill Sergeants?

First of all, you will get singled out in basic training. Like death and taxes, it's going to happen. However, there are many ways you can minimize special attention from Drill Sergeants. The answer to minimizing special attention from Drill Sergeants is to find the middle ground between a boss and a worker.

Finding the Middle Ground

Small Talk. The first thing I recommend after you get assigned to a platoon is to engage in small talk with everyone. Have a conversation with each individual in your platoon. How do you do that? Simply approach them, so they know you made the effort to initiate a conversation. Remember, these other recruits don't know you. So leave at home any shyness or reservation you had in the past about meeting new people. You will be with approximately thirty recruits from all around the country who are in the same situation you are. You can talk to them about where they are from, how many siblings they have, what sports they play, and anything else that comes to mind. During that conversation, be sure to include at least one compliment about them or their hometown. This small talk will make them feel good about themselves, and most of them will like and begin to respect you.

However, a word of warning is in order! If you are a male complimenting a part of a female's body (or vice versa), they could take the compliment in a manner you did not intend. You do not know how sensitive or politically correct the person next to you is going to be, so be aware of the words you use.

Understanding your Drill Sergeant: Now that most of your platoon members respect your personality and friendliness, the next step is to get positive attention from your Drill Sergeants. The best thing you can do is understand the job of a Drill Sergeant. Why would your Drill Sergeant become a Drill Sergeant? Think about this question for a moment.

Put this book down for fifteen seconds and ask yourself that question: *Why would your Drill Sergeant become a Drill Sergeant?*

Why would this individual undergo an intensive training school comprised of ridicule and tough physical fitness standards just to teach a bunch of new recruits? The answer is simple: pride. Pride for one's country and personal pride.

They have been selected to train new recruits to be a part of the toughest, most revered military in the history of the world. You can benefit from this pride. When a Drill Sergeant introduces himself (or herself) to the platoon, he will likely ask every member of the platoon why he/she joined the military. You will be amazed at how many improper responses you will hear.

"Why did you join the military?" shouts the Drill Sergeant.

"I joined for the college money!" someone will answer.

"I needed a job, Drill Sergeant!" is another common response you will hear.

Never, *ever*, respond that way—even if it is true! There are far better answers that will position you in a better light with your Drill Sergeant. I am not telling you to provide a false answer, or to lie, but how to simply answer the question better.

"Why did you join the military?" Asked the Drill Sergeant.

This is your answer: "I joined because I love my country, sir!" or "I want to be a soldier in the U.S. Military, Drill Sergeant!"

These responses demonstrate pride—the same pride a Drill Sergeant has burning inside his soul. When you give your response, your Drill Sergeant will immediately have a connection with you. She or he will never let you *see* that connection, but it will be there.

Gain Respect

To gain respect from your Drill Sergeant, you must do the following three things:

(1) You must be attentive. Pay attention to your body posture and listen to every word of the instructions;

(2) Keep your head up and back straight in class;

(3) Be confident with your answers and respond loudly and correctly to a Drill Sergeant. Speaking softly does not emphasize a person's strength, confidence, or pride.

Chapter 2

Fitness

"I learned that good judgment comes from experience
and that experience grows out of mistakes."

— General Omar N. Bradley

A major portion of basic training focuses on building physical fitness and endurance. During basic training, your company will conduct an organized physical training session every morning, except Sundays. Each physical training session is comprised of three components:

- Warm-up;
- Conditioning;
- Cool-down.

Generally, you will alternate between running days and push-up/sit-up days.

The Army measures your physical fitness and endurance by giving you multiple Army Physical Fitness Tests (APFT) throughout the nine-week basic training cycle. If you do not pass these tests, your Drill Sergeants will restart (recycle) you and you will be required to start basic training all over again.

The APFT has three components:

- Two-minute timed push-ups
- Two-minute timed sit-ups
- Two-mile timed run

You must score a minimum of 50 points in each category to pass an APFT. (Refer to the APFT charts in Appendix A. However, be aware that every so often the standards change.)

In Advanced Individual Training (AIT), which follows basic training, you must score a minimum of 60 points in each category to pass. It does not matter if you're an excellent runner and horrible at push-ups (or vice-versa). A maximum score in one category of an APFT (i.e., push-ups) does not affect the score of a different category (i.e., sit-ups). You must meet the minimum standards in each category. Even if you meet the minimum standards, your Drill Sergeants will not be pleased. You must surpass the minimum standards.

You should have no problem meeting the fitness standards by following the exercise program in this chapter for at least eight weeks prior to basic training. Again, Appendix A lists the APFT standards. The tables mentioned in this chapter are located in Appendix B.

Running Improvement

Running is the only fitness category in the APFT that tests your cardiovascular fitness. Most people have never learned to run properly. However, by learning and applying a few simple techniques, the efficiency of your body movements can increase dramatically. Always try to run with a partner; it is motivating and easier to keep pace with someone running next to you. Just make sure your partner doesn't slow you down. During the APFT, you may choose to run with a partner or alone.

The running program in this chapter is to be performed every other day. You will alternate between sprint days and long-run days. By following this program at least eight weeks prior to basic training, you should have no problems passing (or even maxing) the running portion of the APFT.

Selecting the Proper Running Shoe

The first step in finding the proper running shoe is to determine your foot type. There are three main types of feet: high arch, normal arch, and low arch. To determine which type you are, wet your feet thoroughly and shake off the excess water. Next, step on a dark and dry surface. I recommend a brown paper bag or a piece of smooth wood. The imprint produced will form a shape similar to one of the three shown below in Figure 3:

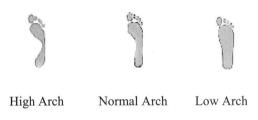

High Arch   Normal Arch   Low Arch

Figure 3: Foot Shapes

Once you determine which foot type you are, you can shop for the proper running shoe. Don't shop for shoes in the morning; your feet swell slightly when you sleep, which could give you a false assumption of your actual foot size.

If you have a highly arched foot, you need a shoe with extra cushioning in the middle area of the shoe (Army and Air Force Exchange Service [AAFES] tag "C").

If you have a normal foot type, your ankles pronate inward as you step. Therefore you will need a shoe with average cushioning (AAFES tag "S"). Do not buy a shoe with extra cushioning in one area or extra motion control features.

If you have a low arched foot, your ankles pronate inward, but more excessively than the normal foot type. Buy a straight or slightly curved shoe, such as a motion control shoe (AAFES tag "M"). AAFES tagged shoes can be found at Post Exchanges (PX).

Stretching

Always stretch before you do any physical exercise. The following stretching techniques will help you properly prepare your body for running:

*Quadriceps
(front of leg)*

Balance yourself against a sturdy object or wall. Grasp your right ankle behind your back with your right hand. Gently pull up with your hand. Figure 4 (on the right) shows a common mistake many people make when trying to perform this stretch. Be sure to pull at the ankle and not pull at the toes. Doing this will reduce the chance of an injury.

Figure 4: Common mistake when stretching the quadriceps.

Keep your head up, stand erect, and do not bend over at the waist. Do not bounce. Hold this stretch for a minimum of thirty seconds for each leg.

Groin Stretch (inner legs)

With your buttocks on the floor place the bottom of your feet together in front of you (Figure 5, next page). Slowly bring your

Figure 5: Proper technique for stretching the groin.

feet as close to your body as possible. Gently grasp your feet and slowly push your knees toward the floor with your elbows. Hold this stretch for a minimum of 30 seconds.

Hamstrings (back of legs)

With your buttocks on the floor, straighten your legs in front of you about 18" apart (Figure 6, next page).

Gently reach for the toe on your right leg with your right arm, and hold this for about thirty seconds. When you are finished, repeat this with the left leg, and hold again for about thirty seconds. This simple exercise will stretch the hamstrings, <u>but do it gently</u>

Figure 6: Proper technique for stretching the hamstrings.

Figure 7: Proper technique for stretching the calves.

and slowly, so you do not risk injuring your low back or pulling a different set of muscles.

Calves
(back and bottom of legs)

Lean against a wall with the left leg behind you (Figure 7). The right leg should be in front of you bearing most of your weight. Keep the heel of the left foot on the floor with the toe pointed forward. Gently move your hips forward toward the wall. The farther forward your hips move, the greater the stretch. Hold for 30 seconds and repeat with the other leg.

Running Technique

Before you begin any running program, you must learn how to run properly. By practicing the various running techniques outlined here, you will greatly improve your efficiency and reduce the risk of injury.

> **Did you Know?**
>
> A stride is calculated by measuring the distance of ten normal sized steps, and dividing the distance you walked by 10.

Below is a list of quick fix running tips you can implement immediately into your running program. If you find that these techniques change your stride significantly, then make your changes gradually. These new techniques could put stress on different muscle groups, which could result in injury until your body adapts to the new running style.

Quick Fix #1

Run straight in a vertical alignment. Your body should be angled forward to the point where you will almost feel like falling over. Be careful not to stick your buttocks out; do so will create improper balance.

Quick Fix #2

Keep your feet on the ground as little as possible. It is common for people to run heel to toe as their foot strikes the ground. Land on the mid-foot, or forefoot if possible. When you land on your heels, you are placing your body's center of gravity behind you. This forces your body to push harder with every step and wastes energy.

Quick Fix #3

Do not bounce when you run. Use your energy to create horizontal and not vertical movement. The less vertical movement you have when running, the more energy you can use to propel your body forward.

Quick Fix #4

Your foot should land under your body when it strikes the ground, not in front of you. By doing this, you will ensure better leverage and balance.

Summary

Quick Fix #1: Run straight in a vertical alignment.

Quick Fix #2: Keep your feet on the ground as little as possible.

Quick Fix #3: Don't bounce when you run.

Quick Fix #4: Your foot should land under your body when it strikes the ground.

Quick Fix #5: Pull your heel toward your buttocks by contracting the hamstring.

Quick Fix #6: Resist the temptation to push off with your toes.

Quick Fix #5

Don't swing your legs back and forth. Instead, when your foot strikes the ground, pull your heel toward your butt by contracting the hamstring. This technique creates a shorter leg arch so your legs get in position faster for the next step without any wasted energy.

Quick Fix #6

Resist the temptation to push off with your toes. By contracting your hamstring muscles (as described in quick fix #5) you will save energy for those long runs.

8-Week Running Program

Running should be done every other day. Getting sufficient rest is just as important as exercising. Resting allows your body to recuperate and allows your muscles to get stronger after a workout.

This running program can be accomplished regardless of your current fitness level. If you find this program too easy, then add some distance and/or speed to the run. Just make sure that you follow the minimum requirements.

This program gives you eight weeks to get in shape for basic training. If you have more time than eight weeks, then take advantage and begin early. If you don't have eight weeks to complete this program, start from the beginning and do what you can. Every little bit helps before you start basic training.

Warm-Up With a Jump Rope

Jumping rope is a great warm-up exercise. It gets your blood flowing, your heart rate up, and your muscles ready for the run. Jumping rope also builds the lower leg muscles that are essential for running. A proper warm-up is outlined in Table 1 and should be followed before every run. If the jump rope gets tangled and you are forced to restart your movement, add the time you stopped jumping to the time limit you are trying to accomplish.

Equipment Needed:

- **Stop Watch**

- **Pedometer**

Initial Assessment

This running program will increase your running distance and improve your running speed. Don't ever fall behind in a run in basic training. If you do, your Drill Sergeant will believe you are unmotivated, and you could lose privileges (such as passes). Before you begin this running program, you need to evaluate your level of fitness. You will need a stopwatch and a pedometer to do so.

A pedometer is a device that attaches to your hip and calculates how far you have run. A pedometer can be purchased at just about any sports store for a few dollars. If you are running on a standard track, a pedometer is not needed. One complete circle around a standard track is one-quarter (¼) mile, or 440 yards.

After you have stretched and elevated your heart rate with jump rope exercises, you can begin your assessment. Use your stopwatch and determine how long it took you to run one mile. One mile equals four laps around a standard track. Look in Appendix A and determine the minimum time you will need on **You can either push yourself hard on your own terms . . .** the APFT (use the 50 point mark). Insert that time in Table 2.

Complete the one-mile run as fast as possible. Log this one-mile run on all three dotted lines in Table 2. Be sure to log your time in seconds. For example, an 8:36 minute one-mile run equals 516 seconds. Next, fill in the blanks to determine your "sprint time goal." The .80 will increase your one-mile jog time by 20 percent.

Since this might be your first time running in a while, do whatever it takes to keep running. <u>Absolutely resist the urge to walk</u>. When you alternate running and walking, your body (and your heart) will not **. . . or be forced to push yourself on your Drill Sergeant's terms.** be able to maintain a consistent rate. If you absolutely must stop running, then walk briskly. You need to keep your heart rate up to increase your fitness level. <u>Stop if you feel pain</u>.

Just remember: push yourself hard on your own terms, or be forced to push yourself on your Drill Sergeant's terms. Take a one-day rest after the one-mile assessment.

Sprint Day

Initially, run ¼-mile. Be sure to beat the sprint time goal (from Table 2). If you run ¼-mile and do not beat the goal, then re-run the ¼-mile. It might sound tough, but again, better to be disciplined on your own terms than on your Drill Sergeant's terms. Once you complete a ¼-mile run, then walk briskly for ¼-mile. You want to keep your heart rate up to increase your stamina. Log your time in Set 1 on Table 3.

After the ¼-mile brisk walk, complete a second ¼-mile sprint, log this time under Set 2. Again, walk briskly for ¼-mile. Repeat three more times until you have completed all five sets. After completion, be sure to stretch and drink water. After two weeks, fill in the evaluation chart (Table 4). Only use the run times in which you surpassed your sprint time goal. If you did not surpass your goal, use the "re-done laps" time instead. Remember, the "re-done laps" are those ¼-mile laps you had to redo because you failed to surpass your sprint time goal.

Once you complete Tables 3 and 4, continue your running program by completing Tables 5 and 6, Tables 7 and 8 and Tables 9 and 10. With each set of tables completed, your sprint goal is calculated (by filling in the evaluation chart) to be 10 percent faster than the previous two weeks. Once the tables are completed, run two miles to the best of your ability. Refer back to Table 2 and compare your new two-mile score with the APFT standard. You will be amazed at the improvement. Be sure to keep an accurate log with the tables. Charting your progress is important and motivational.

Long-Run Day

On long-run days, your goal is to keep your heart rate up for a measured period of time. If your legs are sore, don't run. Replace running with stretching your legs. Be sure to focus on the running techniques outlined in the beginning of this chapter.

Follow Table 11 during long-run days. You are running for a length of time during this session and not necessarily for speed, as you do during sprint days. If you cannot continue running, stop the stopwatch and walk briskly. Continue the stopwatch once you begin running again. Since you are performing the running program every other day, you should alternate between sprint days and long run days.

Figure 8: Proper push-up form—starting position.

(Above) Figure 9: Proper Push-up form (lowered position)

Push-Up Improvement

The push-up is used by the Army to test your upper body strength. There are literally hundreds of exercises you can do to build upper body strength. However, the best way to increase the number of push-ups you can do in two minutes is to actually DO the push-ups.

The push-up program I have set forth below should be performed every other day, along with the sit-up program. Note, however, that practicing both push-ups and sit-ups too often does not allow for muscle recuperation.

Figure 10: Proper technique for stretching the triceps.

Figure 11: Proper technique for stretching the chest.

Figure 8 (page 18) shows the proper starting position for a push-up. Notice the back and legs are straight, the head is up and the arms are at shoulder level. Your body should be lowered to the position as shown in Figure 9 (page 19, top). The upper arms are parallel to the floor and the back and legs remain straight.

Stretching for Push-Ups

The push-up involves numerous upper body muscles, primarily the triceps, chest, and the shoulders. By stretching these muscles before each workout, you will reduce your muscle soreness and your chance of injury.

Triceps (back of arm)

Lift your right arm up over your head with your left hand pushing back on the right triceps just above your right elbow (Figure 10, page 19, bottom). Hold for thirty seconds and repeat with the left arm. This also stretches the shoulders.

Chest

Position your forearm on the edge of a wall or other stationary object (Figure 11, previous page). Place your feet in line with the wall's edge. Lean out and away from the wall's edge. Hold for a minimum of thirty seconds then repeat with the other arm.

Shoulders

Place your right arm behind your back with your right hand reaching toward your left shoulder (Figure 12). Grab your right wrist with your left hand and pull it gently higher. Hold for thirty seconds, then repeat with left arm.

*Improving Push-Up
Performance*

This push-up program is designed to be rigorous, regardless of your current fitness level. The more you put into this program, the

Figure 12: Proper technique for stretching the shoulders.

more you will get out of it. You will be doing both fast and slow push-ups.

Refer to Appendix A to determine the number of push-ups you must complete to pass the APFT (use the 50 point mark). Enter that number at the top of Table 12. After proper stretching, see how many push-ups you can do in one minute. Do these push-ups as quickly as possible, but in a controlled manner. Only those push-ups with correct form should be counted. Remember the number of push-ups you just performed. Drop immediately to your

Figure 13: Proper technique for kneeling diamond push-up.

knees and continue doing push-ups, but this time put your hands close together (as shown in Figure 13 above). This type of push-up is called a kneeling diamond push-up because your forefinger and thumbs form a diamond shape. These push-ups should be done very slowly—three seconds for the downward movement, and three seconds for the upward movement.

Keep doing push-ups until you can't continue. When you are done, enter your numbers in line A and B in Set 1 of Table 12 (enter A for regular push-ups and B for kneeling diamond push-ups). Rest two full minutes and complete another set. Enter those numbers in Table 12, Set 2, lines A and B. Complete a third set and stretch afterward. After three weeks of performing three sets of one-minute timed push-ups, complete three weeks of 1:30 minute timed push-ups. For weeks Seven and Eight, do three sets of two-minute timed push-ups. Perform this workout every other day along with the sit-up program.

Do not be discouraged if by the second or third set your number does not meet the minimum APFT standards. Your muscles will be

Figure 14: Proper sit-up form (starting position).

tired before the sets even start, unlike when you take an APFT test when your muscles are fresh. By the time basic training starts, you will be prepared to meet and exceed the push-up standard.

Figure 15: Proper sit-up form (vertical position).

Sit-Up Improvement

Figure 14 (previous page, top) shows the proper starting position for a sit-up. Notice the legs are bent at a 90-degree angle, the heel is in contact with the floor, and the fingers are interlocked behind the head. During an APFT, a partner will be holding your ankles with his hands. Your body should be raised to the position as shown in Figure 15 (previous page, below). In the vertical position, the base of the neck is above the base of the spine.

During an APFT, raising your body to the vertical position and returning it to the lowered position is considered one full repetition. Similar to the push-up, you can save considerable energy during a fitness test by using gravity to let your body return to the lowered position. However, during practice you can build muscular endurance by lowering yourself slowly to the starting position.

This sit-up program is intense, so <u>stop immediately</u> if you feel any abnormal discomfort, and rest and reduce the intensity.

Stretching for Sit-Ups

The sit-up involves the torso and abdominal muscles. Soldiers often injure their upper quadriceps (leg muscles) by using the wrong muscles to raise them to a vertical position. To thoroughly stretch before a sit-up, perform the stretch described for quadriceps in the running section. Note: sit-ups done improperly can be harmful to the back. The torso extension stretch (Figure 16) will stretch your abdominal muscles and the spine.

Figure 16: Torso extension stretch.

To properly perform the torso extension stretch, lie on your stomach and use your forearms to hold your body weight. Relax and slowly raise your upper body, keeping your waist on the floor. Hold for a minimum of thirty seconds. To increase the intensity of the stretch, place the palms of your hands on the floor, instead of your forearms.

Improving Sit-Up Performance

This eight-week sit-up program is designed to significantly increase the amount of sit-ups you can do in two minutes. This program is not designed to give you a flat six-pack stomach or melt inches off your waist.

Perform this program on the same day as the push-up program. Before starting, get comfortable by placing a towel under your tail bone or use a soft surface, such as a mat, to lie on. Do not use a bulky surface such as a couch or mattress.

Refer to Appendix A to determine the amount of sit-ups you will need to do to pass your fitness test (use the 50 point mark). Enter that number at the top of Table 13. After proper stretching, see how many sit-ups you can perform in one minute. Do these sit-ups as quickly as possible and with correct form. Breathe out on the way up. Remember the number of sit-ups you just performed.

Figure 17: Proper technique for abdominal crunches.

Figure 18: Proper technique for upper half crunches.

Immediately begin abdominal crunches (as shown in Figure 17, previous page). Place your hands behind your head or across your chest. Once your shoulder blades are off the ground, return to the starting position. Perform abdominal crunches until you cannot continue. When you are done, enter your numbers in line A and B in Set 1 of Table 13 (A for regular sit-ups and B for abdominal crunches). Rest two full minutes and complete another set.

This time, instead of performing abdominal crunches, perform upper-half crunches. The mid-point of the sit-up is the starting position for this exercise (Figure 18, above). Enter those numbers in Table 13, Set 2, lines A and C. After three weeks of performing two sets of one-minute timed sit-ups, complete three weeks of 1:30 minute timed sit-ups. For the seventh and eighth weeks, do two sets of two-minute timed sit-ups. Once this eight-week sit-up improvement program is complete, APFT standards will be easily accomplished.

Table 14 outlines exactly what you need to accomplish, day-by-day, for eight weeks. Use Table 14 as a checklist. If you are unable to workout for a day, <u>do not skip the workout</u>! Instead, use it as a day of rest, and pick up the exercise program the next day where you left off.

Tips for Maximizing Your APFT Score

- During an APFT, lowering your body and raising it to the starting position is considered one full repetition. Save energy during a fitness test by using gravity to let your body fall. However, during practice you will want to lower your body in a controlled manner to build muscle.

- When taking an APFT, you may have to wait in a long line before it is time to perform your push-ups or sit-ups. About five minutes before it's your turn, perform just a few push-ups or sit-ups (depending on which portion of the test you're waiting to take). Doing this will increase your blood flow and prepare your muscles for the task at hand.

- Avoid muscle failure during an APFT when doing the push-ups and sit-ups. When your muscles approach failure, rest for a little while, and then start back up again. Be sure to rest in an authorized position, which will be explained to you before the APFT begins.

- Sometimes an APFT grader will not count a repetition for various reasons (i.e., didn't come up high enough on a sit-up, or down far enough on a push-up). When this happens, make a deliberate and obvious attempt to correct your form. Doing this will let the grader know that you heard his remark and the problem is being rectified. Always focus on form. Try not to waste energy on bad repetitions.

- Pace your breathing and speed on the running portion of the test. Many recruits get anxious during the run and take off running full speed (or nearly full speed) when the whistle blows. There are many reasons why you should avoid doing this. By starting slow on the run, you will be passing others one-half mile down the road, which is motivational.

Miscellaneous Exercises

Other than push-ups and sit-ups, there are several miscellaneous exercises you will need to know about before arriving at basic training. Some exercises you do in basic training are common knowledge, such as jumping jacks, military presses (using your eight-pound —16 rifle as a weight) and pull-ups. In basic training, you won't go to a gym and lift weights. Many exercises you do will use your body weight as resistance. This is a good reason to lose weight before basic training starts.

In basic training, you will become very familiar with the following exercises. Practice these exercises at home until you are familiar with the form.

Flutterkicks: Strengthens the Stomach

Lie on your back and place your hands under your buttocks. Raise your feet six inches above the ground with your legs very slightly bent and head off the ground (Figure 19). This is your starting position. To begin the movement, raise one of your legs about 12 to 16 inches. As that leg reaches the top, begin returning it to the starting position as you raise the other leg 12 to 16 inches. Repeat.

Figure 19: Starting position of a flutterkick.

Figure 20: Starting position of overhead claps.

Overhead Claps: Strengthens the Shoulders

Extend both your arms to the side of your body, about shoulder level with your palms facing up (Figure 20, above). Your arms

Figure 21: Starting position of a plank.

should be bent slightly. Raise your arms up and clap your hands above your head. Return them to the starting position and repeat.

Planks: Strengthens the Stomach

Assume the push-up position. Instead of resting on your hands, rest on your forearms (Figure 21, previous page, bottom). Your back should be straight. Hold this position for one minute. After about twenty seconds you will feel your abdominal muscles getting tight. The further you bring your elbows past your head, the more difficult this exercise will become.

Leg Spreaders: Strengthens the Inner Thighs

Assume the flutterkick starting position. Keep your legs slightly bent to reduce back strain. Spread your legs approximately 18 to 30 inches apart. Return your legs to the starting position and repeat.

Ski Jumpers: Strengthens the Legs and Calves

Stand upright, place your hands on top of your head, and your feet together. Jump to the left about 18 inches. As soon as you touch the ground, jump to the right about 18 inches. Repeat. The faster you perform this exercise, the more challenging it will become.

Front-Back-Go: Strengthens the Cardiovascular System

You will need a partner for this exercise. When your partner yells "front," you will begin doing push-ups as fast as possible. After you do push-ups for a while, have your partner yell "back." On the command of "back" you will start doing sit-ups as fast as possible. After some time elapses, have your partner yell "go!" On the command "go," you will run in place with your arms extended in front of you. Your Drill Sergeant will certainly get you acquainted with this exercise.

Toe Touches: Strengthens the Legs

Stand upright with your feet shoulder width apart. Place your hands on your hips. This is the starting position. Begin by bending your legs and touching your ankles. Keep your back straight. Return to the starting position and repeat. Drill Sergeants often refer to this exercise as "dusting your boots."

Donkey Kicks: Strengthens the Legs and Cardiovascular System

Stand upright and interlock your fingers behind your head. This is your starting position. Jump and kick your heels to your buttocks. Repeat. This exercise, also called "mule kicks," is commonly done on gravel and sand to increase difficulty.

Figure 22: Starting position of mountain climbers.

Mountain Climbers: Strengthens the Legs and the Cardio-vascular System

Place your hands on the ground approximately three or four feet in front of your feet. Your back should be naturally arched (Figure 22, previous page). This is the starting position.

Begin the exercise by running in place without moving your hands. Move your knees close to your chest.

Chapter 3

Prepare Yourself Early

"The eyes of the world are upon you. The hopes and prayers of liberty-loving people everywhere march with you."

— General Dwight D. Eisenhower, addressing his men before D-Day, 1944.

To give yourself a major advantage before you depart for basic training, it is imperative that you start thinking and acting like a soldier. This chapter will help you begin that journey.

First, start exercising early in the morning. During basic training, your organized physical training sessions will be conducted in the morning before breakfast. Therefore, a couple weeks before you start basic training, make it a habit to get up at 4:30 a.m. Don't just get up and watch television! Get up and follow the workouts described in Chapter 2 of this book. I want to emphasize what a tremendous advantage this will give you.

Stop munching on chips and cookies. During basic training, there is no snacking. By training your body early to stop snacking, you will help reduce your hunger urges during basic training.

If you smoke or use chewing tobacco, I highly recommend you begin a program to quit immediately. There will be no tobacco products allowed at basic training. It is better to develop a plan to quit on your own terms, rather than the military's terms. Too many recruits come to basic training and experience a variety of withdrawal symptoms. This only makes the already tough nine weeks of vigorous basic training unnecessarily tougher for you.

Put down and step away from those boil-and-eat noodles you are picking up at the market, ten packs for a buck. Throw away the bologna. Instead, cook yourself lean beef, chicken, fish, and pasta dishes. Your body will appreciate the consumption of healthier foods, and this nourishment will compliment the workout plans described in Chapter 2.

> **Did You Know?**
>
> Why do soldiers in the Army workout so early in the morning?
>
> One reason is that if you workout before breakfast, your body uses stored fat as fuel instead of carbs. Thus, you burn more fat by working out before breakfast!

During basic training you will rarely get eight hours of sleep—five to seven hours is normal. Train your body to go to bed about 9:00 p.m. This way, when you get to basic training you won't be lying in bed awake when everyone else is sleeping. Here is another tip: consider the time zone where your basic training will be conducted. If you are on the West coast and you will be training on the East coast, there is a three-hour time difference. Training yourself to go to bed at 9:00 p.m. Eastern Time means going to bed at 6:00 p.m. on the West coast. Likewise, waking up at 4:30 a.m. Eastern Time means waking up at 1:30 a.m. Pacific Standard Time.

Everyone is different, but it generally takes four to seven days to adjust to a new sleep schedule. Will this change be uncomfortable and even frustrating? Yes. But you know that already, and you will adjust and survive—and basic training will be that much easier.

Chapter Summary:

- **Wake up early**
- **Start exercising**
- **Stop snacking**
- **Stop using tobacco**
- **Eat healthy**
- **Adjust your sleeping schedule**

Chapter 4

Phases

"Tomorrow's battle is won during today's practice."

— Samurai maxim

Basic training is composed of three phases, red phase, white phase and blue phase. Each phase has different learning objectives, goals, and privileges. Each phase of basic training will vary slightly depending on where you are stationed. A general description of each phase is listed below.

Red Phase: Weeks 1-3

This phase is known as the total control phase. For the first three weeks of basic training you will not be allowed to sit down at meals (chow) without asking permission. You will take an initial APFT. The Drill Sergeant will be paying particular attention to every detail of your physical and mental condition. Because you

Your Drill Sergeant will test your capability to handle stress.

are reading this book, you will be aware of these details before going to basic training. Also, your physical fitness program will begin every morning. Introductory classes in army values and traditions will be conducted. Your Drill Sergeant will test your ability to handle stress. During the red phase, your only privilege will be a trip to the PX for basic supplies (escorted by a Drill Sergeant, of course).

White Phase: Weeks 4-6

During this phase you will learn basic marksmanship skills. You will learn how to assemble, disassemble, and zero your M-16 rifle. This is the only phase where physical fitness is equally as important as learning about your weapon.

Nearly the entire phase is spent on the range practicing with, what will quickly become your best friend: your M-16 rifle. Your Drill Sergeant will be relatively nice to you during this phase, or I perhaps I should say, *nicer* to you (in a relative sense). Don't be fooled. It is not because they are starting to like you. It is because they are surrounded by about 200 rifles held by recruits who can't use them properly.

You will also take another fitness test and will qualify with your M-16 rifle. In order to qualify, you will have to shoot 23 out of 40 targets of varying distances (not to exceed 300 yards). During the White Phase, you may be given passes which allow you to spend a couple of hours in a designated area without a Drill

---

Did You Know?

There are several types of passes a recruit can be granted. A battalion, brigade, and post pass will allow you to spend time in each of those areas. "Battalion" passes are those that encompass the smallest area, and "post" passes encompass the largest. An off-post pass allows a recruit to go off-post within a certain, limited, area.

Sergeant's supervision. It is common for recruits to go to a movie theater during these two-hour passes.

Blue Phase: Weeks 7-9

During this phase, nicknamed the "total failure" phase, you will be given the End of Cycle Training (EOCT) test. The EOCT will test what you have learned since you began basic training. You will also take your final APFT. You must pass the final APFT or you will be recycled.

During this phase, your Drill Sergeant will be emphasizing your physical fitness. Your morning physical training sessions will be more intense than ever—hence the nickname "total failure." A three-day field training exercise (FTX) will be conducted that will encompass everything you have learned since day one of basic training. This FTX concentrates on leadership development, teamwork skills, and self-discipline.

During the Blue Phase, you may be given an on-post pass (or even an off-post pass) that could last the majority of the day. Beware: any pass can be taken away from an individual or an entire company for poor performance.

You must pass the final APFT or you will be recycled.

Chapter 5

Reception

> "The man who can't make
> a mistake can't make anything."
>
> —Abraham Lincoln

Before basic training begins, you will begin a process called "Reception." At the Reception Center, you will spend about three days with other incoming recruits. These recruits may not be the same recruits who accompany you through basic training. You will be fed very well and get plenty of sleep.

<u>Do not be fooled</u>. When you arrive at your basic training company, this will change immediately.

During the reception process, all recruits go through the same general steps. These steps are as follows:

- Chaplain activities
- Red Cross function

> **You will be fed very well and get plenty of sleep. But don't be fooled . . .**

- Uniform Code of Military Justice
- Processing company policies
- Handling of your personal affairs
- General orientation
- Vision and dental check
- Immunizations (shots)
- Initial pay
- Medical testing
- Interview
- Uniform issue and fitting
- Identification card issue
- Personal records processing

In all likelihood, you will not get a chance to contact your friends and family after your arrival at the Reception Center. Before you leave home, be sure to inform your friends and family you will not be able to call for at least several days.

You should have a bank account set up before you leave for basic training. Bring your account information and an ATM/debit card with you. Direct Deposit is mandatory for military pay. If you don't have a bank account established, one of the first things that will be required of you to do at reception is to establish an account at the local credit union or bank. However, it may be several weeks before the bank can give you a debit card, and this will affect your ability to access your pay. Expect to receive your first paycheck about thirty days after you arrive.

The reception period will not last long, but it will feels like it lasts a long time. There is plenty of waiting around. After the reception process, you will be begging to start basic training. Don't worry, that feeling will only last for about two minutes—until its time to meet your Drill Sergeants.

Chapter 6

Battle Buddies

"There is at least one thing worse than
fighting with allies, and that is to fight without them."

— Winston S. Churchill

"An Army of One" is more than just the Army motto; it is also a lesson to live by in basic training. This chapter discusses that philosophy, and how to apply it during basic training.

One of the most important lessons you will learn in the Army is to look out for your fellow soldiers. To teach you this lesson, your Drill Sergeants will assign you a battle buddy. You will be responsible for how your battle buddy looks, acts, and performs (and vice versa). If your battle buddy does something wrong, then you have done something wrong, too. If your battle buddy isn't wearing an article of clothing correctly, guess who else is to blame? Right—you are.

Do not be surprised if your battle buddy is not the same race, ethnicity, or age as you. Commonly, Drill Sergeants will pair up two individuals who are completely opposite of one another. You must learn how to work closely with someone with a different background.

Before every formation, make sure your battle buddy is wearing his/her uniform properly. If there are buttons on the

It is common for Drill Sergeants to pair up two individuals who are completely opposite of one another.

uniform, make sure they are buttoned. Most importantly, make sure your battle buddy doesn't forget anything for formation (i.e., canteens, paperwork, etc.).

Make a mental note of what your strengths and weaknesses are compared to your battle buddy's. For example, you might be able to get dressed faster than he can, but you might be slower at making your bed. By noticing these small differences, you will be able to give advice to each other. Think as a team. Think as *one*.

Your battle buddy will be someone you will never forget. Make a conscious effort to be tolerant toward that individual. Ask anyone who has attended basic training about this. If they didn't get along with their battle buddy, they didn't have a good experience in basic training. It is really that important.

A good relationship with your battle buddy could make the difference between a miserable or valuable basic training.

Chapter 7

The Gas Chamber

"Veni, Vedi, Vici
(I came, I saw, I conquered)"
—Julius Caesar

Every recruit who goes through basic training will go through nuclear, biological, and chemical (NBC) training. That means you will be subjected to training in the gas chamber.

Worrying about this training can be (and often is) worse than the actual training! Many recruits wonder why they need to go through the gas chamber in the first place. You will be subjected to the gas chamber to gain confidence in your NBC equipment (e.g. protective mask). Confidence in your equipment will mean a great deal if you need to use it in a real life situation.

What is the Gas Chamber?

The gas chamber is a room holding a controlled concentration of CS gas. CS gas (orto-chlorobenzylidene-malononitrile) is more commonly known as tear gas. Tear gas is the active ingredient in Mace™ and used for self defense and for riot control by policeman. Tear gas is an irritant. It irritates mucous membranes in the eyes, nose, mouth, and lungs. The irritating effect causes tearing, sneezing, coughing, etc.

The Process

Usually, during your second or third week of basic training, you will be subjected to the gas chamber. You will have access to your daily schedule and know in advance when you are slated to experience the gas chamber. If you are scheduled to go to the gas chamber in the afternoon, I suggest eating a light lunch. Taking a few breaths of tear gas on a full stomach is not a good feeling.

Before entering the gas chamber, you will be trained on how to fit your protective mask and chemical gear. Learning how to clear your gas mask is very important. Some recruits fail to pay attention to these instructions and regret their lack of attention once inside the gas chamber.

A number of different things can occur while you are in the gas chamber. I will explain to you the most common method Drill Sergeants use to move the recruits through the gas chamber.

You will line up in a group (usually 5 to 15 recruits) outside of the gas chamber door. Your group will be asked to file into the gas chamber. Once inside, you will be joined by one or more Drill Sergeants. The room will be very foggy. The fog you see is CS gas. You may smell it slightly through your mask. You will see a Drill Sergeant with a coffee can next to a table. This coffee can will have a flame inside. This flame is the CS gas burning. A Drill Sergeant will touch your shoulder and ask you to lift your mask and state your name, rank, and social security number. Many recruits get nervous and forget the answers to these simple questions. If you remain calm you will do fine. As the Drill Sergeants touch your

> **"Learning how to clear your gas mask is very important. Some recruits fail to pay attention to these instructions and regret their lack of attention while in the gas chamber."**

shoulder, take in a deep breath, close your eyes, lift your mask, answer the questions in one breath, put your mask back on, and clear the mask. This part of the gas chamber is not difficult if you stay calm.

However, over the years, the Drill Sergeants have learned that recruits accomplish this without inhaling any CS gas. The Drill Sergeants want you to inhale CS gas. They want you to know the importance of chemical gear. Therefore, after everyone in your group finishes stating their names, ranks, and social security numbers, you will be ordered to take off your mask and file out in order without closing your eyes.

The Treatment

As you are exiting the gas chamber, your eyes will be filling with water and your lungs and face will be filling with mucous. The best treatment is air. As soon as you exit the gas chamber, open your eyes. This will seem like a hard task to do, but keeping your eyes open in fresh air will make any discomfort you are feeling dissipate very quickly.

I cannot emphasize enough to not touch your eyes. Touching and rubbing your eyes is the worst thing you can do, but you will have a great desire to do so. Take deep breathes of air with your arms over your head and you will be surprised how quickly the CS leaves your system. In less than one minute, you will be nearly back to normal.

Smile Pretty

Typically, a historian will follow your basic training company for nine weeks. At the end of basic training, this historian will have a book for sale filled with pictures of all the events you recently accomplished. The pictures from the gas chamber are not exactly pictures you want your friends and family to see. You will probably have drool on yourself, and it will look like you just sneezed 47 times in a row and didn't have access to tissues. Therefore, as you exit the gas chamber, look for the historian and head in the other direction. Don't forget to put a pack of tissues in your cargo pocket before you enter the gas chamber!

Chapter 8

Schedule Breakdown

"Never in the face of human conflict has so
much been owed by so many to so few."

— Winston Churchill ("Battle of Britain")

Even though basic training is conducted on many military installations throughout the country, the schedule is remarkably similar. This chapter describes what you will be doing during the nine weeks of basic training.

First, though, let me provide a tip few recruits ever consider: *choose carefully, if you can, where and at what season you attend basic training.* The military is an outdoor sport, and activities are rarely cancelled because of the weather. If you don't like cold weather, don't go to basic training in December in Missouri. If you don't like the heat, stay away from Texas in July. In many cases, your recruiting site determines the location of your basic training. Ask your recruiter.

Week-by-Week Breakdown

Basic training will take eight weeks to complete (not including the reception process). Here is what you will accomplish, and what will be expected of you.

Week 1

You will receive an introduction to the physical fitness program you will perform almost every morning for the next eight weeks. You will be taught various stretches and common military exercises.

You will be assigned an M-16 rifle, and you will learn marching movements (with and without the M-16) called Drill and Ceremonies (D&C).

WEEK 1 TIPS: Pay attention to detail this week, as you will be flooded with information. At the end of the day, write down what you have learned in a small notebook, and review your notes every chance you get.

Week 2

As you continue your physical fitness regimen, you will be introduced to even more exercises than you learned the previous week. The running program will now include wind sprints, which mixes fast sprints with jogs.

You will learn how to assemble, take apart, and clean your M-16 rifle. Various firing positions will be practiced and range procedures will be taught. Your company will train at a bayonet course where you will learn how to fight with a bayonet.

WEEK 2 TIPS: Treat your M-16 rifle like glass. Drill Sergeants hate it when you drop your weapon. It might sound silly, but one thing you can do to care for your weapon better is to name your M-16 rifle. If an object has a name, people tend to give it better care. Commonly, soldiers will name their weapon after their spouse or mother. Then they treat their weapon like they would a loved one.

Week 3

This week is dedicated almost entirely to rifle marksmanship. You will practice firing from various positions, rapid reloading, sight adjustments, and moving with a loaded weapon.

WEEK 3 *TIPS: Tension and stress is high from the previous two weeks and most recruits are starting to feel the effect of being away from their families while looking at the long road ahead. This week, it is very important that you be extra tolerant of others and try and recognize when your friends are feeling depressed.*

Week 4

This week you will qualify with your M-16 rifle. To qualify, you will have to hit 23 out of 40 targets at various distances. The farther the target is from your firing position, the longer the time the target will appear. If you qualify, you will earn one of three badges, marksman (23-30 targets), sharpshooter (31-35 targets), and expert (36-40 targets).

Long road marches, guerrilla exercises, and simulated hand-to-hand combat will accompany your continued physical fitness regimen. During this week, your physical fitness program will most likely include jogging, wind sprints, push-ups, sit-ups, and pull-ups.

WEEK 4 *TIPS: Qualifying is surprisingly easy. The recruits who fail, do so because of nerves. You will most likely wait many hours before it is your turn to qualify. Use that time to review techniques in your head and practice steady breathing.*

Week 5

For part of this week, you will leave the barracks and live in tents while you perform field skills you were taught during the previous four weeks. You will receive instructional classes on first-aid, camouflage techniques, how to set up defensive fighting positions, and how to take cover. You will experience your first night fire exercise at the range, which is a favorite among recruits.

The Drill Sergeants will be inspecting your living area and little slack will be given to those who make mistakes.

WEEK 5 *TIPS: It is common for a recruit to get sick the first time spending the night in the field. Avoid this by using proper field sanitation. Trim your fingernails and toenails before going out to the field. Make sure you have hand sanitizer, baby wipes, and soap handy at all times. Avoid touching your fingers to your mouth, and brush your teeth often. Keep harmful organisms off your boots by applying shoe polish every day.*

Weeks 6 and 7

By now, you are very familiar with what your Drill Sergeants expect of you. Physical training is as intense as ever. You will perform a nighttime tactical road march. A hands-on class called U.S. Weapons will be taught in which you will learn to use machine guns, grenade launchers, and claymore mines. Most recruits leave basic training claiming the class on U.S. Weapons was the most enjoyable day (besides graduation day). A class on map and compass reading will also be taught. The map class will teach you how to identify different types of terrain and determine distances. The compass class will teach you how to determine direction and angles.

Inspections will include a display of field gear (called a TA-50), a thorough barracks inspection, and a wall locker inspection.

WEEKS 6 and 7 TIPS: Take good notes during these two weeks. Many classes are given in a short amount of time. The class on map and compass reading is short and packed with information. A thorough understanding of these two classes are required to graduate, so make sure you understand all the information and study your Smartbook thoroughly.

Weeks 8 & 9

These are the final weeks. Before graduation day, you will finish any unfinished business, such as the series of classes on the seven core values, and prevention of sexual harassment. You will take a final physical fitness test and undergo a Class A uniform inspection.

WEEKS 8 AND 9 TIPS: During these weeks, recruits get excited because basic training is nearly over. That means most recruits get careless with their behavior. Usually, more Article 15's (see Appendix C for a definition) are given out during these weeks then all the other weeks combined.

Watch your behavior and your attitude and you will be graduating shortly.

Chapter 9

Day 1

*"Courage is going from failure to failure
without losing enthusiasm."*

— Winston Churchill

Ask anyone in the military, or anyone with prior military service, to describe his first day of basic training. A smile will appear on his face and he will tell you a story full of remarkable detail. I guarantee you that person was not smiling when he was experiencing these events.

The first day of basic training is not fun, and it is not meant to be. But it is an experience most people look back upon and smile about. Every recruit's first day is a bit different, but generally speaking the same experiences will occur. You will board a bus from the Reception Center. The Drill Sergeants will be yelling at you and banging on windows. Don't worry, they are not allowed to hit you. As you get off the bus (tip: don't be the last one off the bus!) you will be given an impossible task that you will fail several times. Even if your company accomplishes the task perfectly, your Drill Sergeants will still say you have failed. By failing, you will be forced to do physical training, and on your first day, you can be sure you will get plenty of it. The following stories describe what six different soldiers experienced on their first day at basic training.

> **"Every recruit's first day is a bit different, but generally speaking, the same sort of experiences occur."**

Specialist James Burke, Ft. McClellan, July 1996:

"As soon as we got on the bus at the Reception Center, the Drill Sergeants were yelling and screaming at anyone who looked at them or even opened their mouth to talk.

After the short ride, the bus stopped and more Drill Sergeants packed on the bus. They filled the aisle and one of them yelled, "You have exactly thirty seconds to get off the bus." As everyone made a mad dash to the door, recruits were running into Drill Sergeants, which made them even angrier. Of course, you can't file about 150 recruits off a bus that holds 100 people in 30 seconds, so we knew we were in trouble before we even began to file off the bus!

When we were all off the bus, we had to carry our duffle bags with us. The Drill Sergeants would tell us to walk to meaningless points on this field and when we got there, we would have to do exercises because we didn't get there fast enough. The Drill Sergeants would throw our bags on the ground and tell us to pick them up and roll on the muddy ground."

Specialist John Bowman, Ft. Leonard Wood, January 2001:

"At the Reception Center, we were packed on a cattle truck tighter than a can of sardines. The Drill Sergeants were yelling at us for absolutely everything they could: the sun was shining too brightly, or one of them didn't like the smell of the cattle truck.

When the cattle truck stopped, we were filed out, lined-up, and ordered to hold our luggage over our heads. When someone dropped his luggage, we all had to do more exercises, exercises I have never heard of before, like the mountain climbers and donkey kicks [see miscellaneous exercises section in Chapter 2]. Of course, we couldn't do the exercises correctly because we had never heard of them, so that led to yet more exercising. I bet I did one thousand push-ups that day with duffle bags on my back."

Staff Sergeant Misty Mokros, Ft. McClellan, July 1995

"On the bus, we weren't allowed to make a sound. I have never tried so hard in my life to hold in a sneeze. The Drill Sergeants were peering at us, waiting for someone to make a noise.

When the bus stopped, a Drill Sergeant told us to ranger walk off the bus carrying all our gear, and go to the middle of this field where he was pointing. No one knew what a ranger walk was [see Appendix C], so everyone just plowed over each other. Needless to say, we all did plenty of flutterkicks and push-ups for the next hour. After our exercises, we had to line-up our bags in a straight line. If your bag looked slightly out of line, you won a chance to do more exercises."

Sergeant Kerry Ladd, Ft. Jackson, August 2000

"After we loaded on a bus, about ten Drill Sergeants crammed into the isles. They introduced themselves on the way to the barracks. The Drill Sergeants didn't start yelling at us until we got off the bus.

Once they started yelling, we were told to carry our bags up two flights of stairs. We made our way to this large open room where we dropped our bags and had to move these gigantic wall lockers around and arrange them in different configurations per the Drill Sergeant's instructions."

Specialist Dawn Hendrix, Ft. Jackson, August 1997

"We were escorted on a very comfortable bus with only two Drill Sergeants. Everyone was silent the whole ride. Funny thing was, so were the Drill Sergeants. They didn't say a word. When the bus stopped we figured this was when all hell would break loose.

Quite the opposite happened. We were told to carefully exit the bus. When everyone was off the bus there was a large table in front of us with juice and cookies. They sat us down and showed us basic marching skills [see Chapter 12] as we ate junk food right in front of the Drill Sergeants. At this point, I was thinking what a great nine weeks this was going to be!

Once the marching exhibition ended, they asked us nicely to get in formation. I guess everyone was acting a little lax from the sweets because we didn't move fast enough, and all hell broke loose. Drill Sergeants were yelling at us for every little thing and the exercises seemed to last all night."

Specialist Troy Graham, Ft. Benning, July 1993

"We were packed in cattle trucks so tightly we could barely move our arms. A short ride later, the truck stopped. The gate to the cattle truck opened, and when we got off the Drill Sergeants went off. They were yelling at everything and made us file in alphabetical order in under three minutes, while carrying all our bags. Obviously 150 strangers are not going to be able to file in alphabetical order in three minutes (which in Drill Sergeant time is approximately 45 seconds). Therefore, we spent the remainder of the day doing push-ups with duffle bags on our backs."

*   *   *

Did you notice the similarities in each of these stories? In each one, the recruit was given a task he or she was not able to accomplish. Be prepared to fail your first task, and don't let that failure break your spirit!

Chapter 10

Make the Most of Your Meals

"Train hard, fight easy . . . and win.
Train easy, fight hard . . . and die."

— Unknown

During basic training, if you get more than three minutes to eat your meal, consider yourself lucky. Many recruits go to bed hungry at night. But it doesn't have to be this way. Your food consumption can increase dramatically by following these tips:

Eat Smart

If given an option, always choose rice to eat. *Always*. Eat it first, along with the main course. Rice grains expand in your stomach and give you a full feeling. Rice (especially brown rice) is packed with the healthy carbohydrates your body needs to fuel your physical training.

> **"Rice grains expand in your stomach
> and give you a full feeling."**

Think S-A-N-D-W-I-C-H

Whenever possible, make a sandwich out of your meals. For example, let's suppose you are served chili macaroni with mashed potatoes and peas. Instead of trying to cram those little macaroni's on your fork with a pea or two, spread the macaroni on a piece of bread. Then, pile on the mash potatoes and mix in the peas. Army-style mash potatoes can glue just about any two foods together. Top it off with another piece of bread and *voila!*—you have a Dagwood-style sandwich and will be done eating in no time.

Some recruits will laugh at you (except those who bought this book). Just smile in return—because you will be doing so with a full stomach. After you have eaten fully and time runs out, they will be half through and half hungry. You, in turn, will be the one going to bed with a full stomach.

You will be surprised how much quicker it is to eat with your hands than it is to use utensils.

Water . . . Water . . . WATER!

Drink plenty of water.

Many recruits choke trying to eat too much food, too fast. During the nine weeks of basic training, you will see (probably several times) a Drill Sergeant performing the Heimlich maneuver on a choking recruit. This is less likely to happen if you drink water. It lubricates your throat and allows the food to slide down easier. Water is also like an oil for your body. We are, after all, almost entirely made of water, right? So replenish as often as you can to help your body function as well as it can.

> **"Remember: You are not in basic training to taste your food; you are there to EAT IT and get back to training."**

Look For These Foods

Choose meals that are high in protein, such as beef, fish, and chicken. Protein is a building block for muscles and makes you feel full.

Avoid eating sugar. Sugar is filled with empty calories and will leave you feeling hungry.

A Few More Miscellaneous Meal Tips

- The closer your mouth is to your plate, the faster you will eat. Doing this will also keep you out of trouble. You won't feel the urge to talk to anyone, and others won't try and talk to you if your face is six inches away from your plate. You may look like a pig, but you will be a pig with a full stomach.

- Avoid adding salt, pepper, or other sauces to your food. Sauces have little, if any, nutritional value. Squeezing on ketchup or steak sauce only wastes time. You're not there to taste your food; you are there to eat your food and get back to training. You will hear this sentence more than once from your Drill Sergeants.

Chapter Summary (and common sense):

- **Get used to waking up early before you begin boot camp**
- **Start exercising before you begin boot camp**
- **Stop snacking—now**
- **Stop using tobacco—now**
- **Eat healthy**
- **Adjust your sleeping schedule**

- Don't touch, or even look at, any type of dessert. This can be really difficult, but you must not eat junk food during basic training. Despite the fact that it's not healthy for you, it's not worth the exercises your Drill Sergeants will make you do later.

Bon appetit!

Chapter 11

Dress Faster than Superman

"History does not long entrust the care
of freedom to the weak or the timid."

—General Dwight D. Eisenhower

With all the activities the Drill Sergeant schedules during your day, it is no wonder why they make you change clothes so fast. Many recruits are late for formation because they can't seem to get dressed in five minutes (30 seconds, Drill Sergeant time). There are ways to get dressed much faster and never be late to formation.

Prepare Ahead of Time

Believe it or not, you can prepare little things that the vast majority of your fellow recruits will never think of doing. By thinking and planning ahead, you can make your life easier, and give lots of reasons why the Drill Sergeants should pick on someone else other than you.

Your Uniform

First and foremost, make sure your locker is prepared properly. Here is what I mean: in your locker is your uniform. Is it folded or hung up to your Drill Sergeant's specifications? Except for the pants, always make sure the buttons on your uniforms are in fact buttoned! (Keep the top one or two buttons on the pants undone for reasons I will explain later.)

Buttons, Buttons

Before you go to bed each night, make it a habit to check the buttons on your uniforms. Also, it is always good to buy an extra belt, if possible, and keep it looped around the belt holes. You will get two different kinds of battle dress uniforms (BDU's), one for summer and another for winter. You can tell the difference between the two by looking closely at the uniform. If you see faint horizontal white lines on the uniform, you are looking at the summer set of BDUs. If you do not see these white lines, you are looking at the winter set of BDUs. Many recruits mess up by matching summer pants with a winter shirt, or visa versa. Now that you own and are reading this book (hopefully for the third or fourth time), you will <u>never</u> make that mistake. So always pair up the right pants and shirt. Your Drill Sergeants will definitely notice a mixed uniform. And when one of them does—watch out!

Boots

After your uniforms are properly prepared its time to prepare your boots. Your boots come equipped with what's called "quick tie laces." Do the following experiment. While wearing your boot, see how far down you can unlace your boot until you are able to slip your foot out. Lacing up your boot takes a lot of time, and if you are able to slip your foot in and out without unlacing the whole boot, you will save a lot of time.

Now that your uniform and boots are ready to go, you are ready for that next formation!

The Mental Race to your Wall Locker

Once the Drill Sergeant releases you from formation and gives you three minutes to change, it is time to run to your wall locker and find your prepared clothes. But before you do that, let's think about that run to your wall locker. . .

While you are making your way to the locker, you should be mentally thinking of everything you need to bring to formation and where it is in your wall locker. By mentally preparing yourself, you will already know what you need to grab by the time that wall locker flies opens.

Now that you have your prepared boots and uniform out of your wall locker, it is time to get dressed. After taking off your clothes, the first thing that should go on your body is your brown t-shirt. Putting on your brown t-shirt first allows you to not have to tuck it into your pants later.

After the t-shirt comes the socks, followed by the pants. Since you left the top one or two buttons undone, the pants will fit easily around the brown t-shirt that needs to be tucked in. So while everyone else is trying to tuck their brown t-shirts into their pants, you will be lacing up your boots.

By now, you should have everything on but your BDU shirt. I recommend you put this on last because it has your name on it. You will usually be changing with many other recruits in a small room. With all those articles of clothing lying around, it is not uncommon for clothes to get mixed between recruits. Once you put your BDU

Chapter Summary:

- **Prepare your clothes ahead of time**
- **Make sure your uniform matches**
- **Pay attention to what is buttoned—or not**
- **Make your boots slip-on fast**
- **Put your BDU shirt on last**

shirt on, just grab your hat (a.k.a cover), and any miscellaneous gear your Drill Sergeant requested you bring to formation—and you are ready to go!

Chapter 12

How to . . .

"The object of war is not to die for your country,
but to make the other bastard die for his."

—General George S. Patton

This chapter will teach you what you need to know before you arrive at basic training. Recruits rarely know any of the seven "how to" sections you will read about in the following pages. By learning this chapter inside and out *before* you arrive at basic training, you will have an enormous advantage over most of the other recruits.

Who and How to Salute

The act of saluting is a respectful gesture between soldiers. Many civilians (and even some military personnel) do not understand the purpose of the salute. It is important that you do.

The salute's *sole* purpose is to express respect for authority. It is tradition for a lower ranked soldier to salute a higher ranked soldier first—much as it is tradition for a gentleman to hold a door for a lady, and not the other way around.

> ## The salute's sole purpose is to express respect for authority.

Practice your salute in the mirror. A confident salute will show your Drill Sergeants that you are a step above the rest. They will not tell you that, but they will notice—and remember.

Who to salute

It is customary to salute all commissioned officers (see section on rank structure) regardless of rank or sex. Do not salute non-commissioned officers (i.e., sergeants), except in formation. You will learn more about this in basic training. Except in the field, commissioned officers salute each other.

Never salute an officer during field exercises or in combat situations. Saluting an officer in the field is referred to as a "sniper check," because it provides the enemy with an idea of who is in an officer and who is in charge. Enemies love to eliminate leaders.

How to salute

A salute should be confident, like a handshake. While at the position of attention (see basic marching section) or walking, raise your right hand until your index finger touches your hat (a.k.a., cover) brim. If you are not wearing a cover, position your hand above and to the right of your eye putting your right forefinger slightly to the right of your right brow (see Figure 23, next page). If you are wearing eyeglasses and no cover, use the right tip of your glasses as a benchmark. Hold your upper arm horizontally and your forearm inclined at a 45-degree angle. Slightly turn your hand downward so that neither the back of the hand or your palm is clearly visible. At the same time you raise your arm, turn your head to the person or object (i.e., flag) you are saluting. Hold your salute until the salute is returned, then confidently return your arm to your side.

Figure 23: Soldier holding a salute.

Warning: You will see many soldiers adding their own style to a military salute. Do not come up with a style of your own. The salute has strict form and adding style shows disrespect. Drill Sergeants will notice that, too.

How to Wear a Cover

In the civilian world, a baseball-style cap is usually worn with the bill slated upward and folded in an upside down, U shape.

When you receive your hat, or "cover" as you will call it, your Drill Sergeants will be looking for the person who folds and bends

Figure 24: Soldier wearing a cover.

the bill of his cover. The bill of your cover should remain straight in basic training. Once you graduate basic training, your assigned unit might be more relaxed on how you wear your cover.

To properly wear a military cover, place the cover on your head straight and level. The bill of the cover should be parallel to the ground with the base of the bill approximately two inches above the top of the nose (see Figure 24, above).

How to March

While in formation, a leader in front of the formation will give commands. These commands will always come in two parts: the preparatory command, to let you know a command is coming, and the command of execution, to let you know when to execute a movement. In the following section, the preparatory command is

Figure 25: Soldier at attention.

italicized and the command of execution is **bolded**. The leader will give the preparatory command, pause for a quick moment, and then give the command of execution.

Position of Attention: Example of command: **Platoon Attention!**

The position of attention is the most common position you will learn as a recruit. Practice this position in front of a mirror frequently. Use the following steps to correctly stand at the position of attention. (see Figure 25, left).

- Stand straight with your stomach in, chest out and shoulders back.

- Head is facing forward and eyes staring directly ahead.

- Hang arms naturally by the sides of your body.

- Cup your hands and have your thumb touching the first joint of your index finger and alongside the seam of your pants.

- Heels are together and toes are pointed out at a 45-degree angle.

- Do not be lax. Your body should be tense, but not so tense as to strain your body or restrict blood flow.

- Legs are straight, but knees are not locked.

Do not talk, move, sneeze, cough, or even scratch when you are at the position of attention. If rain lands on your face—ignore it. If a mosquito lands on your ear and starts crawling inside—forget about it. If you move at the position of attention, you are showing your Drill Sergeant that you are undisciplined, and Drill Sergeants don't like undisciplined recruits.

Parade Rest—Example of Command **"Parade Rest!"**

This position can only be called from the position of attention; therefore, your starting point will always be the same. When the leader calls "parade rest," execute the following movement:

Figure 26: Soldier at parade rest.

Figure 27: Back of soldier at parade rest.

- Move your left foot about one foot to the left.

- Legs should remain straight with your weight evenly distributed.

- As you move your left foot 12 inches to the left, place your hands in the center of your lower back, just above your belt, with palms facing out (Figure 26).

- Fingers of both hands should be flat and extended outward with your thumbs interlocking (Figure 27, above).

- The right hand should be in the palm of your left hand making only the palm of the right hand visible.

- Your head and eyes should be facing forward.

- Remain silent.

Stand at Ease—Example of command **"Stand at Ease!"**

This position is exactly the same as "parade rest" except your head and eyes will turn toward the person in charge of the formation. During parade rest, your head and eyes remain forward.

Figure 28: Soldier executing "left face."

At Ease—Example of Command **"At Ease!"**

On the command of "at ease," you may move everything but your feet. However, you must remain standing and quiet during this command.

Rest—Example of Command **"Rest!"**

The command of "rest" has the same property as the command of "at ease," except you are now allowed to talk and drink, and you may move everything except your right foot.

Left Face—Example of command **"Left Face!"**

From the position of attention, rotate your left heel 90 degrees to the left, while at the same time raising your right heel and placing it by your left heel (Figure 28, left). Your feet should now look as they would at the position of attention (at a 45-degree angle). Arms should remain by your sides throughout this movement.

Right Face—Example of Command **"Right Face!"**

This command is performed in the same manner as "left face," except the feet switch tasks. This time, raise the left heel and right toe. Rotate your right heel 90 degrees to the right. Place your heels together at a 45-degree angle. Arms remain by your sides as they would at the position of attention.

About Face—Example of Command **"About-Face!"**

This is one of the more difficult commands to execute. When this command is called, move your right toe to the rear and left of your left heel. At this point, there should be a few inches of space between your right toe and left heel. Most of your body weight should be on your left heel, and the right knee should be naturally bent. Turn to the right 180 degrees on the left heel and ball of your right foot.

At the completion of this movement you should be facing the opposite direction of where you started, and be at the position

Figure 29: Soldier executing an "about-face."

of attention (Figure 29, previous page). Your arms remain by your sides.

If possible, ask someone who is, or has been, in the military to execute an about-face. This move is much easier to learn by visual example.

How to Make Your Bunk

A hospital corner is a corner of a made-up bunk in which the sheets have been neatly and securely folded (Figure 30, next page). During basic training you will be required to have a neatly made bunk <u>at all times</u>. A neatly folded bunk will not only keep you out of trouble, but it will also show your Drill Sergeant that you are a "squared away" soldier. Practice making a hospital corner on your own bunk before you leave for basic training.

Steps:

1. Pick up the edge of the sheet about 15 inches from the foot of the bunk;

2. Lift up the sheet so it makes a diagonal fold;

3. Lay the fold on the mattress;

4. Take the part of the sheet that is hanging and tuck it underneath the mattress;

5. Drop the fold, pull it smooth, and tuck that under the mattress as well:

> **A neatly folded bunk will not only keep you out of trouble, but it will also show your Drill Sergeant that you are a "squared away" soldier.**

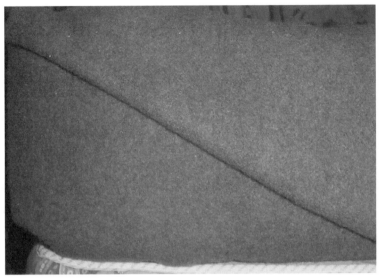

Figure 30: An example of a hospital corner.

6. Turn the top of the sheet over the top of the blanket near where your head rests:

7. Place pillows under blanket and pull sheet tight.

How to Prepare and Eat an M.R.E (Meal, Ready-to-Eat)

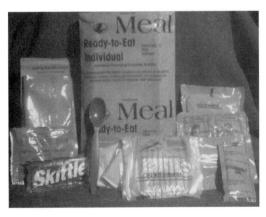

M.R.E's (Figure 31, right) are individual meals soldiers use in the field when no hot chow is available. M.R.E's

Figure 31: An M.R.E. pouch and its contents.

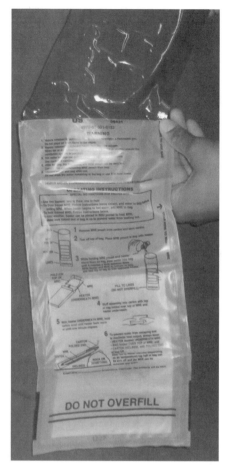

**Figure 32: Placing food into
the heating pouch.**

come in many varieties. Everything from meatloaf with gravy to Thai chicken to vegetarian meals are available.

Inside an M.R.E packet are a series of boxes and small bags. Inside the boxes are packets of food. These packets can be heated with a heater pouch that is included in each M.R.E.

To heat your M.R.E, use the following steps:

1. Tear off the top of the heater pouch. There are two arrows on the pouch, use the top arrow to make your initial tear;

2. Pour a small amount of water in the bag. Do not fill the water past the two black lines about 3 inches from the bottom of the bag.

3. Place your packet of food (Figure 32, above) inside the pouch and make sure the packet reaches the bottom of the bag (so it is flush with the heater);

4. Fold the top of the heater bag;

5. Take the empty box you just took the packet of food from and rip the top 1/3 of it off;

6. Place the pouch in the cardboard box;

7. Lean the box on an object, such as a rock;

8. In about ten minutes remove the packet of food from the box, tear the pouch of food at the notches and enjoy.

How to Polish Your Boots

A well-polished boot will show your Drill Sergeants you are a squared-away soldier. The following list will instruct you on how to get that perfect shine on your boots. Follow these steps:

1. Wash your hands to remove all of the oil and dirt. It is difficult to clean a boot with dirty hands.

2. Unlace and clean the boot. In order to get the dirt and dust off the tongue the laces must be removed. Take an old toothbrush or soft bristled brush and wipe off all the dirt. Be sure to get the tongue, and the side of the sole. Dirt commonly collects where the sole meets the leather of the boot. A toothbrush will get this dirt out easily.

3. Buy a large tin of shoe polish (Kiwi™ brand is common and works well). Open the tin by twisting the metal clip on the side. Use a soft cotton cloth (an old t-shirt works well) or even your bare fingers. Dip the cloth or your fingers into the polish and apply in a circular motion. Use thin layers of polish. Pick a section of the boot to polish. The toe of the boot will shine the best.

4. Buff the polish. Take a clean soft cloth about 8 to 12 inches long. Wrap a piece of the cloth around your index and middle finger. Lightly, in a circular motion, wipe the polish off. At first, you

---

Equipment Needed

- **Black shoe polish**
- **Soft bristled brush**
- **Soft cotton cloth**
- **Toothbrush**

might think you'll never get a shine. After you repeat steps 3 and 4 several times, a glossy shine will appear.

5. Pick a different section of the boot and repeat steps 3 and 4.

There are many variations to shining a boot that are just as effective as the method described above. Experiment, watch what others find success doing, and find a method that works for you.

How to Ace Inspections

There are many inspections a recruit will have to pass in basic training. These inspections are arduous and detail oriented. A recruit will have shoe inspections, locker inspections, bunk inspections, and equipment inspections. Often, your Drill Sergeant will give you a sheet that contains specifications for each of these inspections. Each of these inspections vary according to where and when you attend basic training. However, with a little elbow grease and ingenuity, you can ace any inspection from your Drill Sergeant.

Shoe Inspections

For shoe inspections, always make sure your shoes are perfectly aligned. You will have at least one pair of running shoes, a couple pairs of combat boots, and one pair of Class A dress shoes. Whether your Drill Sergeant requires your shoes to be aligned under your bunk or next to your locker, you can use the floor tiles as a guide. Floor tiles and hardwood floors create a straight line in the floor. Align the toes of all your shoes along this line. To perfectly align the shoes, get on your knees and situate your body in front of the shoes. Look straight down and move the toes of the shoes up to the line. Move over and repeat the same procedure for the next pair of shoes. If you were to just kneel in front of all the shoes and align them at once, they will not be straight, and your Drill Sergeant will notice.

Locker Inspections

The number one important tip for passing your locker inspection is to always maintain a clean locker. Often, the locker inspections are a surprise, so always expect one.

Every article of clothing on hangers should be centered and hung in the same direction. Fold the sleeves across the chest. Place three fingers between the tops of each hanger to make sure the hangers are perfectly spaced. If you have a mirror in your locker, it should be utterly free of smudges. Belts should be rolled or folded according to your Drill Sergeants' specifications. It is wise to buy an extra belt that you keep rolled or folded. Then, you can wear one and always have one ready to be inspected. If your belt will not stay rolled or folded properly in the locker, color a rubber band black with a marker. Since your belt is black, the rubber band will hardly show. Place the rubber band on the area of the belt that allows the belt to stay in place. Also, the ends of the belt should be black; if brass is showing, that means the black has worn away. Do not let the brass of the belt show. If the brass is showing, color it with a black marker.

Bunk Inspections

Before making any hospital corner (see Chapter 12 on how to make your bunk), make sure all the sheets have no wrinkles or folds. Look underneath your mattress and tuck in any remaining bunk sheets so they are not hanging down. Pick off any lint or debris on the covers. When you are done making your bunk, the sheets should appear tight.

Equipment Inspections

Before you graduate basic training, you will be required to return all the equipment (i.e., Kevlar®, flack vest, poncho, etc.) in the same condition it was issued to you. When scrubbed with a toothbrush, AAFES™ dandruff shampoo is great at getting out sweat stains and leaving your equipment smelling fresh. Use a black marker to color in any buttons that have brass showing. After cleaning your equipment, get your battle buddy to check it over as if he were inspecting the equipment. Often, your battle buddy will find something you missed.

How to Relieve Stress

This is a little different than the other topics covered in this chapter, but it is just as important. During the nine weeks of basic training, your stress will rise, tempers will be short, and spirits low. If someone tries to provoke a fight, do *not* take the bait. Not only will fighting invoke disciplinary action (such as an Article 15, which will become a part of your permanent record), but it will add stress and additional duty.

Sometimes it will seem your Drill Sergeant is trying to antagonize fights between recruits. Perhaps sometimes they do. But there is a purpose for everything a Drill Sergeant does. They want to see how you handle stress. Then they will teach you how to deal with stress. At the end of basic training, your entire platoon will act like one person. You will know more than you want to know about each person in your platoon. These new relationships will create a great deal of stress. *Know that going in.*

A helpful way to relieve stress is to write letters to loved ones. Sometimes, especially at the beginning of basic training, you will seem like you are far away from anyone who cares about you. Writing a letter is therapeutic. It will help you organize your thoughts, think about your loved ones, and vent frustrations. Encourage a response in your letters. To most recruits, mail call is the best part of the day.

Another helpful way to relieve stress is to attend religious services. During basic training, you will be allowed to attend religious services (if you desire). Many recruits who have never stepped foot in a church or temple find themselves never missing a service in basic training. At the very least, attending a service gets you out of the barracks and away from the Drill Sergeants—even if it is only for a couple hours.

Chapter 13

Study Guide

"Train hard, fight easy . . . and win.
Train easy, fight hard. . . . and die."

—Unknown

Starting day one, the Drill Sergeants will have every minute of every day of your basic training cycle planned. Your days will be filled with physical fitness, classes, combat activities, etc. You will get one hour every day to prepare for the following day's activities. Most recruits will spend that entire hour shining their boots to meet their Drill Sergeants' strict standards. Other recruits will study their Smartbook and sacrifice the quality job on shining their boots.

Listed below are some of the most common aspects of basic training that recruits spend time studying in order to sacrifice shiny boots. Study these before you arrive at basic training, and you won't need to sacrifice shiny boots for study time.

Rank Structure

The Army has two main routes of rank you can pursue (Figure 33, next four pages): the sergeant route and the officer route. Rank is worn on the collar of a shirt, and on the cover. Generally speaking, an officer plans the details of a mission, and the sergeants

Figure 33 U.S. Army Rank Structure

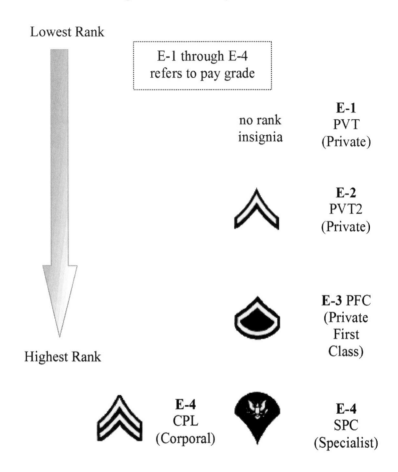

Lowest Rank

E-1 through E-4
refers to pay grade

no rank insignia

E-1
PVT
(Private)

E-2
PVT2
(Private)

E-3 PFC
(Private First Class)

Highest Rank

E-4
CPL
(Corporal)

E-4
SPC
(Specialist)

Lowest Rank

Figure 33. U.S Army Rank
Structure (Continued)

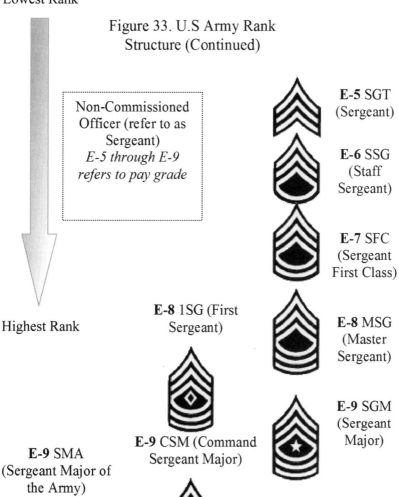

Non-Commissioned
Officer (refer to as
Sergeant)
E-5 through E-9
refers to pay grade

E-5 SGT
(Sergeant)

E-6 SSG
(Staff
Sergeant)

E-7 SFC
(Sergeant
First Class)

Highest Rank

E-8 1SG (First
Sergeant)

E-8 MSG
(Master
Sergeant)

E-9 SGM
(Sergeant
Major)

E-9 CSM (Command
Sergeant Major)

E-9 SMA
(Sergeant Major of
the Army)

Lowest Rank

Figure 33. U.S Army Rank
Structure (Continued)

Commissioned
Officers (refer to as sir
or ma'am)
*O-1 through O-11
refers to pay grade*

Highest Rank

O-7 BG
(Brigadier
General)

O-8 MG
(Major
General)

O-9 LTG
(Lieutenant
General)

O-10 GEN
(General)

O-11 GOA
(General of
the Army)

O-1 2LT
(Second
Lieutenant)
gold

O-2 1LT
(First
Lieutenant)
silver

O-3 CPT
(Captain)
silver

O-4 MAJ
(Major)
gold

O-5 LTC
(Lieutenant
Colonel)
silver

O-6 COL
(Colonel)

Lowest Rank

Figure 33. U.S Army Rank
Structure (Continued)

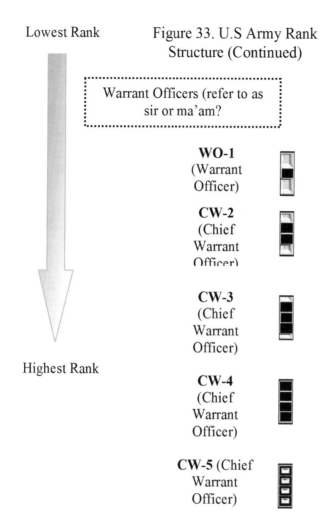

Warrant Officers (refer to as
sir or ma'am?

WO-1
(Warrant
Officer)

CW-2
(Chief
Warrant
Officer)

CW-3
(Chief
Warrant
Officer)

Highest Rank

CW-4
(Chief
Warrant
Officer)

CW-5 (Chief
Warrant
Officer)

carry out those details. Sergeants are known as the backbone of the military. As you begin your military career, you will start out as a private, or if you have enough college credits, a specialist. Later, as you gain time (i.e., experience) in the military, you will be promoted to a higher rank. Several major factors determine if and when you will be promoted.

One factor considered for a promotion is time in service. Time in service is determined by how long you have been in the military. Another factor considered for a promotion is time in grade. Time in grade is determined by how much experience you have at your current rank. Another major factor considered for a promotion will be your leadership skills. Leadership skills are generally determined by awards you earn. Each award has a specific number of promotion points assigned to it. It is possible to earn awards in basic training along with promotion points.

Immediately after basic training ends, call your assigned unit (your recruiter will give you the contact information). Usually, after six months, and maybe even earlier, you may be eligible for a promotion.

How the Army Organizes its Troops

Squad—Approximately 8-12 soldiers. Several squads form a Platoon.

Platoon—Approximately 24-48 soldiers. Several platoons form a Company.

Company—Approximately 100-200 soldiers. Several companies form a Battalion.

Battalion—Approximately 700-800 soldiers. Several battalions form a Brigade.

Brigade—Several thousand soldiers. Several brigades form a Division.

Division—Tens of thousands of soldiers.

Seven Core Values

During your nine weeks of basic training, you will learn and re-learn the seven Army core values. Each of the seven core values will have a one- to two-hour lecture associated with it.

During this lecture, you will sit in a classroom perfectly still with your back straight. The Drill Sergeants will turn the lights down and turn the heat up. They will make the classroom so comfortable that you will want to fall asleep. In fact, there will always be several recruits who will fall asleep in class. <u>I highly recommend you do not fall asleep in class</u>. If you do fall asleep, the entire company will get "smoked" (See Appendix C for definition) because of your actions.

Learning these core values prior to basic training will provide you with a significant advantage. Here are the seven core values:

Loyalty—Bear true faith and allegiance to the U.S. Constitution, the Army, your unit and other soldiers.

Duty—Fulfill your obligations.

Respect—Treat people as they should be treated.

Selfless Service—Put the welfare of the nation, the Army, and your subordinates before your own.

Honor—Live up to all the Army values.

Integrity—Do what's right, legally and morally.

Personal Courage—Face fear, danger, or adversity (physical or moral).

The first letter in each word is highlighted in **bold** and *italics* to help you better remember these important core values. If you read the letters in italics from top to bottom, the seven core values form the word LDRSHIP. You can remember LDRSHIP because it resembles the word "LEADERSHIP."

Soldier's Code

You will have to memorize the following code word for word:

I. I am an American soldier—a protector of the greatest nation on earth—sworn to uphold the Constitution of the United States.

II. I will treat others with dignity and respect and expect others to do the same.

III. I will honor my Country, the Army, my unit and my fellow soldiers by living the Army values.

IV. No matter what situation I am in, I will never do anything for pleasure, profit, or personal safety which will disgrace my uniform, my unit, or my country.

V. Lastly, I am proud of my country and its flag. I want to look back and say that I am proud to have served my Country as a soldier.

Phonetic Alphabet

To ensure a clear transmission of your voice over a radio, the phonetic alphabet is used. Instead of saying a letter, you say the name that corresponds to the letter (Table 15, next page). For example, the grid coordinates HJ86101359 will be read as follows (you will learn more about grid coordinates in basic training):

H J 8 6 1 0 1 3 5 9

Hotel Juliet eight six one zero one tree fife niner

Numbers are spoken, as shown in Table 16 (see page 90).

TABLE 15: PHONETIC ALPHABET			
Letter	**Phonetic Equivalent**	**Letter**	**Phonetic Equivalent**
A	Alpha	N	November
B	Bravo	O	Oscar
C	Charlie	P	Papa
D	Delta	Q	Quebec
E	Easy	R	Romeo
F	Fox	S	Sierra
G	Golf	T	Tango
H	Hotel	U	Uniform
I	India	V	Victor
J	Juliet	W	Whiskey
K	Kilo	X	X-Ray
L	Lima	Y	Yankee
M	Mike	Z	Zulu

| TABLE 16: PRONUNCIATION OF MILITARY NUMBERS ||
NUMBER	PRONUNCIATION
1	One
2	Two
3	Tree
4	Four
5	Fife
6	Six
7	Seven
8	Eight
9	Niner
10	One Zero

Military Time (24-Hour Clock)

Civilian time does not exist in basic training. In basic training, you will only use military time. Military time runs on a 24-hour clock as opposed to a 12-hour civilian time clock. Therefore, in order to convert civilian time to military time, simply add 12 hours to every hour past noon. For example, 4:00 p.m. in military time is 1600 hours (12 + 4 = 16) in military time. Table 17 (next two pages) shows you how to convert civilian time to military time.

When you write the date in the military, it should be expressed as day/month/year. For example, April 2, 2004 is 02Apr04.

TABLE 17: HOW TO READ MILITARY TIME		
CIVILIAN TIME	MILITARY TIME	PRONUNCIATION
12:01 A.M.	0001	zero zero zero one
1:00 A.M.	0100	zero one hundred hours
2:00 A.M.	0200	zero two hundred hours
3:00 A.M.	0300	zero three hundred hours
4:00 A.M.	0400	zero four hundred hours
5:00 A.M.	0500	zero five hundred hours
6:00 A.M.	0600	zero six hundred hours
7:00 A.M.	0700	zero seven hundred hours
8:00 A.M.	0800	zero eight hundred hours
9:00 A.M.	0900	zero nine hundred hours
10:00 A.M.	1000	ten hundred hours
11:00 A.M.	1100	eleven hundred hours
12:00 noon	1200	twelve hundred hours
1:00 P.M.	1300	thirteen hundred hours
2:00 P.M.	1400	fourteen hundred hours
3:00 P.M.	1500	fifteen hundred hours
4:00 P.M.	1600	sixteen hundred hours

CIVILIAN TIME	MILITARY TIME	PRONUNCIATION
5:00 P.M.	1700	seventeen hundred hours
6:00 P.M.	1800	eighteen hundred hours
7:00 P.M.	1900	nineteen hundred hours
8:00 P.M.	2000	twenty hundred hours
9:00 P.M.	2100	twenty-one hundred hours
10:00 P.M.	2200	twenty-two hundred hours
11:00 P.M.	2300	twenty-three hundred hours
12:00 midnight	2400	twenty-four hundred hours
8:36 A.M.	0836	zero eight thirty six
11:52 A.M.	1152	eleven fifty two
12:06 P.M.	1206	twelve oh six
3:11 P.M.	1511	fifteen eleven
10:41 P.M.	2241	twenty-two forty one

General Orders

You will have to memorize and recite every word of these general orders in basic training. The general orders are as follows:

1st General Order

I will guard everything within the limits of my post and quit my post only when properly relieved.

2nd General Order

I will obey my special orders and perform all of my duties in a military manner.

3rd General Order

I will report violations of my special orders, emergencies, and anything not covered in my instructions, to the commander of the relief.

Out of all the chapters in this book, this one might be the most important: <u>read and memorize the content carefully</u>. Commit this information to memory. I suggest you make flash cards, and have you friends quiz you with them.

If you take this chapter seriously, and do what I suggest, all of this information will be easily recalled. When you get to basic training, you will be far ahead of most recruits in this respect.

Chapter 14

What Do I Take With Me to Basic Training?

"One cannot simultaneously prevent and prepare for war."
—Albert Einstein

"What should I take to basic training?"

This is a common question, and one that too many recruits don't think about deeply until just before leaving for basic training. If you are leaving in the morning and trying to get your affairs in order the night before, it is too late. There are many things you can do to help make your experience in basic training easier.

Financial Matters

Before you leave for basic training, make sure your financial affairs are taken care of. How are your bills going to be paid? Do you have enough money in your account to take care of your outstanding obligations until you get a paycheck from Uncle Sam? Some recruits arrange for someone they trust to oversee their financial and personal obligations while they are away. Usually this is a family member, like a parent or brother or sister. In some cases, you might want to grant someone a Power of Attorney for your financial accounts. This gives a third party of your choice legal authority to handle your affairs during your absence. However, before you take such a step, make sure and consult with an attorney first.

> **Did You Know?**
>
> There are two types of Power of Attorney, general and specific. General Power of Attorney grants someone significant power. A specific Power of Attorney might be the route to take if you want someone to handle only specific portions of your financial or personal obligations.

Non-Financial Matters

Take a few minutes and jot down some of your non-financial responsibilities (like mowing the grass, feeding your pets, etc.). Make sure you have someone designated to cover each of these responsibilities. Table 18 (next page), provides a few examples of non-financial obligations. Be sure to have a back-up plan should your original plan fail. Also, be sure to explain to your employer when you will be leaving, how long you will be gone, and a relative's phone number in case information needs to be relayed to you.

What to Bring to Basic Training

Your luggage should be limited to one suitcase or duffle bag. Civilian clothes can be packed, but only take a bare minimum—two or three outfits at the most. Use the following checklist as you pack for basic training.

Below are three lists: one for everyone; one especially for female recruits, and a third miscellaneous list everyone can use. Study them, understand them, and bring everything (*everything*) you can. It's not much, but it will help.

For everyone (male and female):

- Plane and bus tickets
- Orders (several copies)
- Form 1199 (direct deposit)
- Meal tickets
- All Military Entrance Processing Station (MEPS) documents
- A copy of your birth certificate
- Six pairs of underwear (white)

TABLE 18: NON FINANCIAL RESPONSIBILITIES		
Responsibility	**Action**	**Secondary Action**
Mow the lawn.	Every Saturday the neighbors will do it.	Neighbors are to call a lawn mowing service.
Feed the pet/take the pet to vet appointments.	A relative or friend can care for the pet.	A pre-designated pet sitter will be called.
Special occasions for loved ones.	Pre-pay for a gift (i.e. flowers) and arrange for a company to deliver the gift on a certain date.	Send a letter or type an e-mail to the company before the occasion.
Miscellaneous chores throughout house (i.e., vacuum, change air filters)	A relative or friend can do the chores.	A pre-designated cleaning service will be called.
Emergencies	Leave local points of contacts posted on the refrigerator and give a wallet-sized card to a neighbor with emergency contact information on it.	

- A pair of comfortable running shoes
- Two locks (combination, no padlocks)
- Eyeglasses band (if you wear eyeglasses)
- 6 pair of white, calf-length socks (no insignia or logos)
- Black marker
- Extra white cotton t-shirt (you can shine your boots with it)
- Toiletries (use a small black bag to told these toiletries)
- Toothbrush/case.
- An extra toothbrush to shine your boots with
- Hairbrush or comb
- Shaving cream
- Disposable razors with blades
- Two washcloths and towels
- Deodorant
- Shower shoes (all black with no insignia)
- Dental floss
- Shampoo/conditioner in *one* bottle (a small bottle if you're a male; you are not going to have much hair)
- Soap with case

For Women:

- Undergarments
- Panties (cotton)
- Bras
- One full slip
- Flesh-tone nylons/pantyhose
- ¼" or less (in diameter) earrings (gold, silver, pearl, or spherical diamond). Earrings can be worn on Class A uniforms only.

Miscellaneous items

- Long distance calling cards
- Small box of laundry detergent (best in a zip lock bag)
- Stamps (lots of them)
- Stationary

- Insect repellent
- Cough drops. You will get sick at basic training and a sore throat will most likely be your worst symptom.
- A small notebook

What *Not* to Bring to Basic Training

There are many things you definitely should not take with you to basic training. Here are several examples:

- Family members. (No, I am not kidding; some recruits will bring their cousins and grandparents; don't be one of them)
- Contact lenses
- Pets
- Weapons*
- Vehicles
- Pocketknives*
- Obscene/pornographic material*
- Playing cards
- Dice
- Tobacco products
- Batteries (D size only allowed) for flashlight
- Facial hair (Shave your beard and mustache *before* you arrive)
- Alcoholic beverages
- Non-prescription drugs
- Prescription drugs (only allowed with letter from doctor, including birth control pills)

* Items such as weapons, pocketknives and pornographic material are known as contraband, and will be confiscated as soon as you arrive at the Reception Center.

Chapter 15

Top 15 Most Common "Do Not's" for Recruits

"If it moves, salute it; if it doesn't move, pick it up;
and if you can't pick it up, paint it."

—-Anonymous

As you might imagine, there are countless things you should not do during basic training. Some are obvious, but it is surprising how many new recruits do not use common sense when making decisions like this.

The following list comprises the top 15 most common problems for recruits in basic training. <u>Memorize this list</u>!

1. Do *not* talk when you're not supposed to—especially while eating or in formation.

2. Do *not* chew gum.

3. Do *not* use an electric razor.

4. Do *not* shave your head.

5. Do *not* fall asleep in class.

6. Do *not* call your M–16 a gun (call it a rifle).

7. Do *not* say "sorry" or "thank you" to a Drill Sergeant.

8. Do *not* scratch, cough, or sneeze while in formation.

9. Do *not* put your hands in your pockets for any reason *except* to quickly retrieve something (like a tissue).

10. Do *not* remove food from the mess hall.

11. Do *not* lie on your bed unless told otherwise to do so.

12. Do *not* call a Drill Sergeant "Sir" or "Ma'am." Only officers are called Sir (or Ma'am, if the officer is a female).

13. Do *not* say ten or eleven. Say one-zero, one-one respectively, and so on.

14. Do *not* bend, fold, or wear your cover indoors.

15. Do *not* show your palm while holding a salute. Showing your palm means you are giving up.

There are many other things you should *not* do during basic training. However, these fifteen examples are the most common mistakes made by new recruits. Don't reinvent the wheel when others have already learned the hard way.

Remember to memorize this list, and your life will be (at least somewhat) easier during basic training.

Chapter 16

Interview with a Drill Sergeant

"Leadership is the art of getting someone else to do
something you want done because he wants to do it."

—General Dwight D. Eisenhower

Drill Sergeants.

Just the name sends shivers down a new recruit's spine (and for
good reason, as you will soon find out firsthand). What is a Drill
Sergeant if not a relentless, harsh, persistent machine that will do
anything within his power to diminish a recruit's self-esteem and
self-respect. Right?

Well . . . No. None of this is really true.

Drill Sergeants are thought of this way for a reason: because
they act this way. As a recruit, you must remember Drill Sergeants
are humans, too. When Drill Sergeants are acting relentless and
pushing you to try harder, they are simply doing their job—and
doing you a favor.

Picture this scenario: You arrive at basic training where Drill
Sergeants greet you with a smile. They carry your luggage upstairs
and introduce you to your maid who will make your bed and shine
your boots. You are then introduced to your Richard Simmons

look-a-like "exercise motivator," who will help you shed those unwanted pounds while listening to music of your choice in a comfortable environment. What kind of military would we be if this scenario was anywhere near reality?

Because there are many misconceptions about Drill Sergeants, I decided to include this interview to demonstrate that Drill Sergeants are indeed human, and that there is a method to their madness. Believe it or not, they are trying to bring out the best in you.

I sat down recently with Sergeant First Class (SFC) Jason Seno to discuss common concerns recruits have about basic training. SFC Seno was not only a Drill Sergeant, but also a Senior Drill Sergeant. He is highly revered for his phenomenal physical fitness capabilities, and is the very definition of a model soldier. He has seen thousands of recruits move through basic training, and is about to share with you some of his knowledge.

The Interview

Q: What personality traits are more likely to make a recruit successful in basic training?

A: The personality trait of a successful recruit would be one who abides by all of the Army core values (loyalty, duty, respect, selfless service, honor, integrity, and personal courage), and being motivated. All of the Army core values you will learn from your Drill Sergeants. They will integrate these values into your training and teach you what they mean and how to live by them. As far as motivation is concerned, the Drill Sergeants are masters at motivating even the most unwilling souls into doing there their biding.

Q: What personality traits are more likely to make a recruit unsuccessful in basic training?

A: Quitting! Giving up is the one thing Drill Sergeants will not tolerate. If a recruit quits, and loses their intestinal fortitude, they are not only giving up on themselves, but are failing their fellow recruit! That is the quickest way to get you and your battle buddy killed in a combat situation.

Q: What major differences, if any, do you see between male and female recruits?

A: Most female recruits don't have the bad habits that most male recruits have before they enter the military. Female recruits are easier to train in Basic Rifle Marksmanship (BRM) because most of them have not fired a weapon before. Also, female recruits generally listen better to instructions. On the other hand, most male recruits have an easier time with the physical portion of basic training.

Q: Name a few important things a recruit can do to avoid negative attention from a Drill Sergeant.

A: Not doing what your told, and not doing something when and how you are suppose to do it. Also, a lack of motivation or showing false motivation will get any recruit negative attention. That is the quickest way for a recruit to get the whole Drill Sergeant hoard down on them. If a soldier is not living by the Army core values and / or not in accordance with (IAW) Uniform Code Of Military Justice (UCMJ), that, too, will be dealt with on a legal level. It will not only affect your military and civilian career, but your pocket book as well.

Q: How does a soldier qualify to become a Drill Sergeant, and how long can a Drill Sergeant remain a Drill Sergeant?

A: First, a recruit has to complete Basic and Advanced Individual Training (AIT). Then, a soldier has to achieve the rank of sergeant, staff sergeant, or sergeant first class. Once the basic standards are met, then becoming a Drill Sergeant happens one of two ways. The first (if you are active duty in the Army), is to become selected by the Department of the Army (DA). You then go to a Drill Sergeant course that is six weeks long. If you graduate, you will receive your hat and be stationed at a basic training post for up to three years. The other way to achieve Drill Sergeant status is, if you are in the Army Reserves, be transferred to a Drill Sergeant unit. Once in the unit, you have to go to a pre-course and then the Drill Sergeant course. The Drill Sergeant course for Reserves can be done in two-week blocks or a six-week course. You can remain a Drill Sergeant in the reserves as long as you meet all the Army standards and can perform your Drill Sergeant job.

Q: Prior to arriving at basic training, what are three things a recruit can focus on that would greatly increase his or her chance of success (e.g. fitness, learn rank structure, etc)?

A: The three most important things a soldier needs to focus on are: physical fitness and proper training of physical fitness, chain of command/rank structure, and mental preparation to undergo the life changing event that will transform you from civilian to soldier.

Q: What exercise or activity during basic training has the highest failure rate for recruits, and how would you recommend a recruit approach this task?

A: Males and female recruits have different physiological make-ups. They are not equal in the different physical tasks that the military requires them to accomplish. Overall, preparation has the highest failure rate. You will not find the day-to-day tasks that the military requires you to accomplish in any workout video or gym. My recommendation is to physically and mentally train yourself, with a friend for motivation, by following a structured training program that is designed around the military physical training program. That way you will not only physically prepare yourself for basic training; you will also mentally prepare yourself for the Drill Sergeant.

The Drill Sergeant will be everywhere you go, and everywhere you turn.

Chapter 17

Tips for Success

"Live for something rather than die for nothing."
— General George S. Patton

The following list contains numerous tips you will should know *before* beginning basic training. Remember, you can log into www.ultimatebasictraining.com for more tips.

- *Designate cleaning chores for each member of the platoon.*

  It's best to designate two chores to two recruits at a time. That way, if one person slacks off, the other recruit is responsible for getting both chores done.

- *Learn how to use a floor buffer.*

  Pay attention to detail. You will hear your Drill Sergeants mention "attention to detail" constantly.

- *Keep your locker organized at all times.*

Whenever you touch something inside your locker, put it back where it belongs.

- *Prepare to Clean it*:

  At the completion of basic training, you will have to thoroughly clean your equipment (TA-50). AAFES Dandruff Shampoo is fantastic at getting dirt and sweat stains out of your TA-50 equipment.

- *Learn Military Time*:

  Learning military time can be made much easier if you get a watch with an alarm that displays military time.

- *Initial It*!

  Write your name or initials on absolutely everything you bring to basic training.

- *Lock It*!

  Always, *always*, always secure (lock) your wall locker, even if you leave the room for only 30 seconds.

- *Socks and Underwear*:

  You cannot have too many pairs of both. So bring plenty of socks and underwear (at least one week's worth). Finding time to do laundry in basic training is difficult.

- *Tuck Them*:

  Keep your shoelaces tucked inside your boots.

- *Be Considerate*:

Make a conscious effort to be considerate of others, especially in times of high stress.

- *Prepare Your E-mail List in Advance:*

  Gather all of your friends and families' e-mail addresses and add them to an address book on your e-mail provider. Then, if you get to a computer during one of your passes at basic training, you can write one e-mail and send it to all your friends and family at once.

- *Phone Cards (Don't Leave Home Without Them):*

  Buy lots of phone cards before you leave for basic training. It is much easier to have one handy when a phone opens up and you get time to place a call.

- *Be the Early Bird:*

  Wake up a few minutes earlier than the other recruits. Doing this will allow you to not be quite so rushed, and will reduce some of your stress.

- *Think "Mature":*

  Try to be the mature recruit in the platoon. The other recruits will respect you more than the others and will be more willing to help you when you are in need.

- *Carry a Razor:*

  Males should carry a razor with you in their uniform pocket. A Drill Sergeant may notice you missed a spot shaving, and will require you to correct the problem on the spot.

- *Hair Length:*

For females, hair extending past the bottom edge of the collar is prohibited. Get it cut by a professional before you leave for basic training.

- *Be Quiet!*

  Never speak out unless you are asked to talk. If no one has requested you speak—don't!

- *Never Lean*:

  Do not lean on walls or other objects. If you have acquired this habit as a civilian, start breaking yourself of it—now.

- *Smiling is Forbidden*:

  Do not ever smile when a Drill Sergeant is talking to you! Even if he compliments you or pretends to be making small talk, never let your guard down and smile. *Ever.*

- *Expect the Unexpected*:

  Do not be upset when you have to wake up in the middle of the night to do exercises. This is a common tactic Drill Sergeants use to increase your stress level. Expect the unexpected and you will never be disappointed.

- *Your Luggage*:

  Take only plain luggage to basic training. Why? Drill Sergeants love to pick on recruits who show up with luggage decorated with flowers, designs, or bright colors. You are asking to stand out—and you will.

- *Carry your Rifle—Everywhere*:

  Whenever your Drill Sergeants have you carry your rifle,

always keep it with you at all times. If a Drill Sergeant finds it unattended (and they will be looking for those recruits who leave them lying around, as many will), you will get smoked.

- *Expect the Worse*:

  Always expect the worse. If a Drill Sergeant says you will receive an overnight off-post pass one weekend, <u>do not expect it until you actually get it</u>. Often, your pass will be taken from you for something someone else did wrong.

- *March With your Left Foot First—Always*:

  Every time you start a marching movement (i.e., forward march), your first step will always be with your left foot. Practice it, and get used to it.

- *The Beat is also on the Left Foot:*

  You will be required to sing cadences while marching. Remember: The beat is always on the left foot. Practice that, too.

*   *   *

By studying this list and drilling these tips into your head, you will be well ahead of the game when you arrive at basic training because you will avoid many of the mistakes that so many recruits make.

Chapter 18

Changes

"One cannot simultaneously
prevent and prepare for war."

– Albert Einstein

The basic training regime you will undergo is based upon decades of trial and error. The training program focuses on combat tactics and survival, which were largely derived from the experiences gained from the Vietnam War and World War II. However, for the first time in decades, changes are underway.

The upcoming changes in the basic training schedule reflect situations a recruit might experience in Iraq or Afghanistan. A recruit is now taught how to identify and deal with suicide bombers, wage urban combat, and detain hostile civilians.

Currently these changes are being tested in the "pilot" phase at Fort Knox, Fort Benning, and Fort Jackson. The traditional basic training program has a three-day field training exercise (FTX). The new pilot program includes a 23-day FTX. During these 23 days, recruits are trained on:

- How to identify and counter remote-controlled bombs, known as improvised explosive devices (IEDs).

- How to identify and deal with Suicide bombers.
- Convoy tactics and ambush retaliation. Recruits learn to strategically place sandbags inside vehicles to protect against bombs, grenades, and other weapons.
- Combat fighting and urban combat. Recruits learn tactics for fighting enemies who blend in with civilians.
- First-aid training. Recruits undergo a more intensive first-aid course than they did in the past.
- The use of heavy weapons (i.e., machine guns).
- Rules of engagement (knowing when to show and use force toward an enemy).

Rest assured, even with future changes in the basic training regimen, the lessons you learn from this book will still apply. *The Ultimate Basic Training Guidebook* was written to be "timeless," and the pages you are now reading have been updated to reflect that. No matter how much the training schedule changes, every bit of knowledge you obtain from this book will still apply.

Chapter 19

Frequently Asked Questions

"If a nation expects to be ignorant and free . . .
it expects what never was and never will be."

— Thomas Jefferson

I have been fielding calls and emails from people all over the country since the appearance of the first edition of this book.

"Which branch of service is best for me?"

"What does it mean when you say . . . "

"Can I do so-and-so in the military?"

It did not take long before I started hearing and reading many of the same questions—over and over again. These are important questions, and they are obviously on the minds of many people about to enter basic training.

As a result, I decided to include some of the most common themes recruits have asked questions about regarding basic training or joining the military.

Q. Are Drill Sergeants allowed to hit you?

A. Drill Sergeants look and act intimidating. However, they are not allowed to physically harm you.

Q. What is the general difference between the branches of service?

A. For most people, deciding which branch of service to join isn't difficult. Perhaps you come from a family with a long tradition of joining the Marines, or you would like to follow in father's footsteps and join the Navy.

Military family tradition is certainly well acknowledged in American society. However, each person is different. Based on your particular interests and qualifications, you may be better suited for a particular branch of service no one else in your family has considered. Remember, joining the military isn't like applying for a job: you can't just quit if you don't like it. You are signing a contract and taking an oath. Make your decision based on your *interests* and do what will make you happy. The military is not a good place to be miserable.

Here is a brief synopsis on the various military service branches:

Marines: For all intents and purposes, Marines are considered riflemen first. In basic training, they receive more marksmanship training than any other branch of service. Also, Marine basic training is longer than the other branches. The Marines have an incredible ability to convert their dollar power into combat power, as they do not have a big budget like the Air Force. So, in summary, if you are joining the military to be in on the action, to be on the front lines, and to shoot your weapon, the Marines might be the best choice for you.

Army: The Army has the second most intense basic training regimen (after the Marines). Three of the nine weeks of basic training are devoted to marksmanship. Soldiers in the Army have the ability to lead or defend against an assault. In the Army, a soldier can pick from literally hundreds of MOS's (Military Occupational Specialties). The training you receive from your MOS often transfers well into civilian jobs.

Navy: The Navy, although more lax than the Marines and Army regarding marksmanship, is deep rooted with traditions and customs. If you like to travel, the Navy might be your best option. If you are a family man, you might want to consider the time you'll spend away from your family should you join the Navy. On the other hand, if you're single, the Navy can be a terrific opportunity for you to explore other countries and cultures.

Air Force: The US Air Force is certainly an impressive compilation of machinery and technology. If you are good with computers and electronics, you might want to consider the Air Force. The Air Force has the best housing units of all the other branches. As far as educational requirements, the Air Force is the most difficult to get into. Without a high school diploma, you chances of getting into the Air Force are slim.

Coast Guard: The Coast Guard is a branch of service that sometimes goes unnoticed. The coast guard has about 25 enlisted jobs to choose from. Their responsibilities are vast, ranging from search and rescue missions, maritime law enforcement, and even environmental protection. To join the Coast Guard, you will need a high school diploma. Basic training in the Coast Guard takes eight weeks to complete.

Q: I have heard that many people get sick in basic training. Is this true?

A: Oddly enough, it is nearly inevitable that you will catch something during basic training. Just about everyone does—whether it's a head cold or a sore throat. You will most likely not be at your physical best in boot camp. Just expect that.

Why? Basic training is too crowded and too fast paced for your body to get enough rest. Your body will be stressed for a long period of time, and this will break down your immune system. I had such a bad sore throat at boot camp, I was unable to swallow sometimes when I woke up. Further aggravating the sore throat was the Drill Sergeant's relentless obsession with having us recruits yell everything at the top of our lungs. To reduce your chances of getting sick, drink a lot of water (I mean *many* glasses each day) and always wash your hands before you eat. Often you will be eating in the field, so always carry a wet napkin in your pocket.

Q: What is the meaning of HUA, or HOOAH?

A: This is one of the most widely used military acronyms of all times, and yet no one can agree on its spelling, origin, or even on its meaning. Undoubtedly it will be the first acronym you will hear as you arrive at Basic Training. You will hear thousands of new soldiers utter the acronym, whisper it, shout it. and even sing it. But what exactly does it mean?

I have scoured the Internet, referenced books, and asked military scholars. Only one conclusion has come from my research: there is no known origin for the meaning of "hooah." There are many *opinions*, but there is no single definitive answer.

Urbandictionary.com claims the term "hooah" was originally used by the British in the late 1800s in Afghanistan, and was more recently adopted by the United States Army to indicate an affirmative or a pleased response. Many books call "huah" an "all-purpose" expression. Perhaps the broadest definition I have come across in my research might very well be the best, and even most comical, definition. According to the Department of Military Science and Leadership, University of Tennessee, Hooah "refers to or means anything except no."

So while military experts and personnel disagree on the term, spelling, origin, and meaning of HUA, huah, hooah, etc, it is widely used throughout the military. Regardless of its meaning, a common aspect encompasses each of the definitions for this term. The term is an expression of high morale, confidence, motivation, and spirit.

Q: What is the ASVAB

The Armed Services Vocational Aptitude Battery (ASVAB) is a multi-aptitude test maintained by the Department of Defense that tests four areas: Arithmetic Reasoning, Word Knowledge, Paragraph Comprehension, and Mathematics Knowledge. Your scores determine how you qualify for certain Military Occupational Specialties (MOS). For more information, and even free practice tests, go to www.military.com

Q: Can I choose my job specialty after basic training?

Your job specialty is called an MOS. If the MOS you desire is available, you can certainly enroll. However, if the job you desire isn't available, you can enlist in the Delayed Enlistment Program. The Delayed Enlistment Program is an agreement to enter basic training at a specific time in the future, when the MOS you desire is available. You must qualify for the MOS you select, and you do so by scoring at a certain level on the ASVAB.

Q: What qualifications would I need to join the Military?

Every military branch requires the following:

1) U.S. citizenship or permanent residency (i.e., a green card if a non-citizen);

2) A high school diploma or equivalent (i.e., GED)

3) Good health;

4) A minimum score on the ASVAB;

5) A minimum age of 17 and a maximum age of 35;

6) No criminal record;

7) A minimum height of five feet for males, and four feet, ten inches for females. There is also a maximum height of six feet, eight inches for both male and female potential recruits.

Read this Book Again

If you have read this book carefully up to this point, and are preparing physically for your new life in the military, you should be ready for basic training. You will be able to show your Drill Sergeants and your fellow recruits you are a squared-away soldier. The knowledge you obtain from this book, if you put it to proper use, will lead to awards, promotion points, higher rank, and increased pay.

By following the fitness program outlined in this book, you will be far ahead of most of the other recruits. When you arrive at your basic training installation, you will be issued a TRADOC Pamphlet 600-4 IET Soldiers Handbook (a.k.a., Smartbook). You will use this Smartbook like Hewey, Dewey, and Louie use the Junior Woodchuck Guidebook in the Ducktales® cartoon. The Smartbook will be your reference for *everything*.

Your Drill Sergeants will notice someone who is prepared for basic training. They will show you no favoritism, however, so do not expect any. If the Drill Sergeants are doing their job correctly, you will never be able to tell they like or dislike you. It may be tough to imagine at times, but Drill Sergeants are humans, too.

Each of them went through basic training just like you. Do not show fear, do not show individuality, and do not show or demonstrate indecisiveness. Show them you can follow orders, handle stress, and be a leader.

Basic training can be a rewarding experience and challenge. You will leave your nine weeks of training with stories and friends that will stay with you forever. You will be proud of yourself and your country when you graduate from basic.

By joining the U.S. military, you have answered the highest call of citizenship. There will undoubtedly be times during basic training when you feel helpless, or times you might believe you cannot do anything right. During these times, you must keep telling yourself you are being mentally and physically molded into the most fit, disciplined, and technologically advanced soldier in modern history.

You are being transformed into a soldier.

You are becoming an Army of one.

Army Physical Fitness Training Charts

To locate the points earned for push-ups and sit-ups, find the number of repetitions performed in the left-hand column. Then, move along that row and locate the intersection of the soldier's appropriate age column. Do the same process to locate the points earned for the two-mile run. If a run time falls between two point values, the lower point value should be used.

Push-Up Standard*

AGE GROUP	17-21		22-26		27-31		32-36		37-41		42-46	
Repetitions	M	F	M	F	M	F	M	F	M	F	M	F
77					100							
76					99							
75			100		98		100					
74			99		97		99					
73			98		96		98		100			
72			97		95		97		99			
71	100		95		94		96		98			
70	99		94		93		95		97			
69	97		93		92		94		96			
68	96		92		91		93		95			
67	94		91		89		92		94			
66	93		90		88		91		93		100	
65	92		89		87		90		92		99	
64	90		87		86		89		91		98	
63	89		86		85		88		90		97	
62	88		85		84		87		89		96	
61	86		84		83		86		88		94	
60	85		83		82		85		87		93	
59	83		82		81		84		86		92	
58	82		81		80		83		85		91	
57	81		79		79		82		84		90	
56	79		78		78		81		83		89	
55	78		77		77		79		82		88	
54	77		76		76		78		81		87	
53	75		75		75		77		79		86	
52	74		74		74		76		78		84	
51	72		73		73		75		77		83	
50	71		71		72	100	74		76		82	
49	70		70		71	99	73		75		81	

AGE GROUP	17-21		22-26		27-31		32-36		37-41		42-46	
Repetitions	M	F	M	F	M	F	M	F	M	F	M	F
48	68		69		69	98	72		74		80	
47	67		68		68	96	71		73		79	
46	66		67	100	67	95	70		72		78	
45	64		66	99	66	94	69	100	71		77	
44	63		65	97	65	93	68	99	70		76	
43	61		63	96	64	92	67	97	69		74	
42	60	100	62	94	63	90	66	96	68		73	
41	59	98	61	93	62	89	65	95	67		72	
40	57	97	60	92	61	88	64	93	66	100	71	
39	56	95	59	90	60	87	63	92	65	99	70	
38	54	93	58	89	59	85	62	91	64	97	69	
37	53	91	57	88	58	84	61	89	63	96	68	100
36	52	90	55	86	57	83	60	88	62	94	67	98
35	50	88	54	85	56	82	59	87	61	93	66	97
34	49	86	53	83	55	81	58	85	60	91	64	95
33	48	84	52	82	54	79	57	84	59	90	63	94
32	46	83	51	81	53	78	56	83	58	88	62	92
31	45	81	50	79	52	77	55	81	57	87	61	90
30	43	79	49	78	50	76	54	80	56	85	60	89
29	42	77	47	77	49	75	53	79	55	84	59	87
28	41	76	46	75	48	73	52	77	54	82	58	86
27	39	74	45	74	47	72	51	76	53	81	57	84
26	38	72	44	72	46	71	50	75	52	79	56	82
25	37	70	43	71	45	70	49	73	51	78	54	81
24	35	69	42	70	44	68	48	72	50	76	53	79
23	34	67	41	68	43	67	47	71	49	75	52	78
22	32	65	39	67	42	66	46	69	48	73	51	76
21	31	63	38	66	41	65	45	68	47	72	50	74
20	30	62	37	64	40	64	44	67	46	70	49	73
19	28	60	36	63	39	62	43	65	45	69	48	71
18	27	58	35	61	38	61	42	64	44	67	47	70
17	26	57	34	60	37	60	41	63	43	66	46	68
16	24	55	33	59	36	59	39	61	42	64	44	66

AGE GROUP	17-21		22-26		27-31		32-36		37-41		42-46	
Repetitions	M	F	M	F	M	F	M	F	M	F	M	F
15	23	53	31	57	35	58	38	60	41	63	43	65
14	21	51	30	56	34	56	37	59	39	61	42	63
13	20	50	29	54	33	55	36	58	38	60	41	62
12	19	48	28	52	32	54	35	56	37	59	40	60
11	17	46	27	50	31	52	34	54	36	57	39	58
10	16	44	26	49	29	50	33	52	35	56	38	57
9	14	43	25	49	28	49	32	50	34	54	37	55
8	13	41	23	48	27	49	31	49	33	53	36	54
7	12	39	22	46	26	48	30	49	32	51	34	52
6	10	37	21	45	25	47	29	48	31	50	33	50
5	9	36	20	43	24	45	28	47	30	48	32	49

*Standard as of February 1999

Sit-Up Standard*

AGE GROUP	17-21	22-26	27-31	32-36	37-41	42-46
Repetitions	M/F	M/F	M/F	M/F	M/F	M/F
82			100			
81			99			
80		100	98			
79		99	97			
78	100	97	96			
77	98	96	95			
76	97	95	94	100	100	
75	95	93	92	99	99	
74	94	92	91	98	98	
73	92	91	90	96	97	
72	90	89	89	95	96	100
71	89	88	88	94	95	99
70	87	87	87	93	94	98
69	86	85	86	92	93	97
68	84	84	85	91	92	96
67	82	83	84	89	91	95
66	81	81	83	88	89	94
65	79	80	82	87	88	93
64	78	79	81	86	87	92
63	76	77	79	85	86	91
62	74	76	78	84	85	90
61	73	75	77	82	84	89
60	71	73	76	81	83	88
59	70	72	75	80	82	87
58	68	71	74	79	81	86
57	66	69	73	78	80	85
56	65	68	72	76	79	84
55	63	67	71	75	78	83
54	62	65	70	74	77	82
53	60	64	69	73	76	81

AGE GROUP	17-21	22-26	27-31	32-36	37-41	42-46
52	58	63	68	72	75	80
51	57	61	66	71	74	79
50	55	60	65	69	73	78
49	54	59	64	68	72	77
48	52	57	63	67	71	76
47	50	56	62	66	69	75
46	49	55	61	65	68	74
45	47	53	60	64	67	73
44	46	52	59	62	66	72
43	44	50	58	61	65	71
42	42	49	57	60	64	70
41	41	48	56	59	63	69
40	39	47	55	58	62	68
39	38	45	54	56	61	67
38	36	44	52	55	60	66
37	34	43	51	54	59	65
36	33	41	50	53	58	64
35	31	40	49	52	57	63
34	30	39	48	50	56	62
33	28	37	47	49	55	61
32	26	36	46	48	54	60
31	25	35	45	47	53	59
30	23	33	44	46	52	58
29	22	32	43	45	50	57
28	20	31	42	44	49	56
27	18	29	41	42	48	55
26	17	28	39	41	47	54
25	15	27	38	40	46	53
24	14	25	37	39	45	52
23	12	24	36	38	44	51
22	10	23	35	36	43	50
21	9	21	34	35	42	49

*Standard as of February 1999

2-Mile Run Standard*

AGE GROUP	17-21		22-26		27-31		32-36		37-41	
Time	M	F	M	F	M	F	M	F	M	F
12:54										
13:00	100		100							
13:06	99		99							
13:12	97		98							
13:18	96		97		100		100			
13:24	94		96		99		99			
13:30	93		94		98		98			
13:36	92		93		97		97		100	
13:42	90		92		96		96		99	
13:48	89		91		95		95		98	
13:54	88		90		94		95		97	
14:00	86		89		92		94		97	
14:06	85		88		91		93		96	
14:12	83		87		90		92		95	
14:18	82		86		89		91		94	
14:24	81		84		88		90		93	
14:30	79		83		87		89		92	
14:36	78		82		86		88		91	
14:42	77		81		85		87		91	
14:48	75		80		84		86		90	
14:54	74		79		83		85		89	
15:00	72		78		82		85		88	
15:06	71		77		81		84		87	
15:12	70		76		79		83		86	
15:18	68		74		78		82		86	
15:24	67		73		77		81		85	
15:30	66		72		76		80		84	
15:36	64	100	71	100	75		79		83	
15:42	63	99	70	99	74		78		82	
15:48	61	98	69	98	73	100	77		81	
15:54	60	96	68	97	72	99	76	100	80	
16:00	59	95	67	96	71	98	75	99	80	

AGE GROUP	17-21		22-26		27-31		32-36		37-41	
16:06	57	94	66	95	70	97	75	99	79	
16:12	56	93	64	94	69	97	74	98	78	
16:18	54	92	63	93	68	96	73	97	77	
16:24	53	90	62	92	66	95	72	97	76	
16:30	52	89	61	91	65	94	71	96	75	
16:36	50	88	60	90	64	93	70	95	74	
16:42	49	87	59	89	63	92	69	94	74	
16:48	48	85	58	88	62	91	68	94	73	
16:54	46	84	57	87	61	91	67	93	72	
17:00	45	83	56	86	60	90	66	92	71	100
17:06	43	82	54	85	59	89	65	92	70	99
17:12	42	81	53	84	58	88	65	91	69	99
17:18	41	79	52	83	57	87	64	90	69	98
17:24	39	78	51	82	56	86	63	90	68	97
17:30	38	77	50	81	55	86	62	89	67	96
17:36	37	76	49	80	54	85	61	88	66	96
17:42	35	75	48	79	52	84	60	88	65	95
17:48	34	73	47	78	51	83	59	87	64	94
17:54	32	72	46	77	50	82	58	86	63	94
18:00	31	71	44	76	49	81	57	86	63	93
18:06	30	70	43	75	48	80	56	85	62	92
18:12	28	68	42	74	47	80	55	84	61	92
18:18	27	67	41	73	46	79	55	83	60	91
18:24	26	66	40	72	45	78	54	83	59	90
Time	M	F	M	F	M	F	M	F	M	F
18:30	24	65	39	71	44	77	53	82	58	89
18:36	23	64	38	70	43	76	52	81	57	89
18:42	21	62	37	69	42	75	51	81	57	88
18:48	20	61	36	68	41	74	50	80	56	87
18:54	19	60	34	67	39	74	49	79	55	87
19:00	17	59	33	66	38	73	48	79	54	86
19:06	16	58	32	65	37	72	47	78	53	85
19:12	14	56	31	64	36	71	46	77	52	85
19:18	13	55	30	63	35	70	45	77	51	84

AGE GROUP	17-21		22-26		27-31		32-36		37-41	
19:24	12	54	29	62	34	69	45	76	51	83
19:30	10	53	28	61	33	69	44	75	50	82
19:36	9	52	27	60	32	68	43	74	49	82
19:42	8	50	26	59	31	67	42	74	48	81
19:48	6	49	24	58	30	66	41	73	47	80
19:54	5	48	23	57	29	65	40	72	46	80
20:00	3	47	22	56	28	64	39	72	46	79
20:06	2	45	21	55	26	63	38	71	45	78
20:12	1	44	20	54	25	63	37	70	44	78
20:18	0	43	19	53	24	62	36	70	43	77
20:24		42	18	52	23	61	35	69	42	76
20:30		41	17	51	22	60	35	68	41	75
20:36		39	16	50	21	59	34	68	40	75
20:42		38	14	49	20	58	33	67	40	74
20:48		37	13	48	19	57	32	66	39	73
20:54		36	12	47	18	57	31	66	38	73
21:00		35	11	46	17	56	30	65	37	72
21:06		33	10	45	16	55	29	64	36	71
21:12		32	9	44	15	54	28	63	35	71
21:18		31	8	43	14	53	27	63	34	70
21:24		30	7	42	12	52	26	62	34	69
21:30		28	6	41	11	51	25	61	33	68
21:36		27	4	40	10	51	25	61	32	68
21:42		26	3	39	9	50	24	60	31	67
21:48		25	2	38	8	49	23	59	30	66
21:54		24	1	37	7	48	22	59	29	66
22:00		22	0	36	6	47	21	58	29	65
22:06		21		35	5	46	20	57	28	64
22:12		20		34	4	46	19	57	27	64
22:18		19		33	3	45	18	56	26	63
22:24		18		32	2	44	17	55	25	62
22:30		16		31	1	43	16	54	24	61
22:36		15		30	0	42	15	54	23	61
22:42		14		29		41	15	53	23	60

AGE GROUP	17-21		22-26		27-31		32-36		37-41	
22:48		13		28		40	14	52	22	59
22:54		12		27		40	13	52	21	59
23:00		10		26		39	12	51	20	58
23:06		9		25		38	11	50	19	57
23:12		8		24		37	10	49	18	56
23:18		7		23		36	9	49	17	56
23:24		5		22		35	8	48	17	55
23:30		4		21		34	7	48	16	54
23:36		3		20		34	6	47	15	54
23:42		2		19		33	5	46	14	53
23:48		1		18		32	5	46	13	52
23:54		0		17		31	4	45	12	52
24:00				16		30	3	44	11	51
24:06				15		29	2	43	11	50
24:12				14		29	1	43	10	49
24:18				13		28	0	42	9	49
24:24				12		27		41	8	48
24:30				11		26		41	7	47
24:36				10		25		40	6	47
24:42				9		24		39	6	46
24:48				8		23		39	5	45
24:54				7		23		38	4	45
25:00				6		22		37	3	44
25:06				5		21		37	2	43
25:12				4		20		36	1	42
25:18				3		19		35	0	42
25:24				2		18		34		41
25:30				1		17		34		40
25:36				0		17		33		40
25:42						16		32		39
25:48						15		32		38
25:54						14		31		38
26:00						13		30		37
26:06						12		30		36

AGE GROUP	17-21		22-26		27-31		32-36		37-41	
26:12					11		29		35	
26:18					11		28		35	
26:24					10		28		34	
26:30					9		27		33	

*Standard as of February 1999

Workout Logs

Full size downloadable workout logs are available at www.ultimatebasictrainingguidebook.com. An explanation on how to use Tables 3-10 can be found in Chapter 2 under the Sprint Day subsection.

To properly follow Table 11, remember, you are running for a length of time not necessarily for speed.

An explanation on how to use Tables 12 and 13 can be found in Chapter 2 under the Improving Push-Up Performance and Improving Sit-Up Performance subsection, respectively.

Use Table 14 as a checklist. This table outlines exactly what you need to accomplish, day-by-day, for eight weeks. If you are unable to workout for a day, do not skip the workout, just use it as a day of rest and pick up where you left off the next day.

Table 1. Jump Rope Program

Weeks 1 and 2		Weeks 3 and 4	
Time Limit	Style	Time Limit	Style
1 minute	feet together	2 minutes	feet together
rest 45 seconds		rest 45 seconds	
1 minute	feet together	2 minutes	alternating legs
rest 45 seconds		rest 45 seconds	
2 minutes	feet together	1 minute	left foot only
		rest 45 seconds	
		1 minute	right foot only
Weeks 5 and 6		**Weeks 7 and 8**	
Time Limit	Style	Time Limit	Style
2:30 minutes	feet together	3:00 minutes	feet together
rest 1 minute		rest 1 minute	
2:30 minutes	alternating legs	3:00 minutes	feet together
rest 1 minute		rest 1 minute	
1:30 minute	left foot only	2:00 minutes	feet together
rest 1 minute		rest 1 minute	
1:30 minute	right foot only	2:00 minutes	feet together

Table 2. Initial Running Assessment

Date: _____

Minimum APFT Score: _____
Time (seconds)

1-mile assessment = _ _ _ _ _

Estimated 2-mile assessment = _ _ _ _ _ x2= _____

1/4-mile sprint time goal = _ _ _ _ _ /4= _____ x.80= _____

Spring Logs

(Tables 3, 5, 7, and 9)

Table 3. Sprint Day Log (Weeks 1 and 2)

_____ Sprint Time Goal (carried over from Table 2)

Date	Sprint	Goal Beat?	Sprint	Goal Beat?	Sprint	Goal Beat?
Set 1						
Set 2						
Set 3						
Set 4						
Set 5						
re-done laps						
re-done laps						

Date	Sprint	Goal Beat?	Sprint	Goal Beat?	Sprint	Goal Beat?
Set 1						
Set 2						
Set 3						
Set 4						
Set 5						
re-done laps						
re-done laps						

Date	Sprint	Goal Beat?	Sprint	Goal Beat?	Sprint	Goal Beat?
Set 1						
Set 2						
Set 3						
Set 4						
Set 5						
re-done laps						
re-done laps						

Table 5. Sprint Day Log (Weeks 3 and 4)						
_____ Sprint Time Goal (carried over from Table 4)						
Date	Sprint Goal Beat?		Sprint Goal Beat?		Sprint Goal Beat?	
Set 1						
Set 2						
Set 3						
Set 4						
Set 5						
Set 6						
re-done laps						
re-done laps						
Date	Sprint Goal Beat?		Sprint Goal Beat?		Sprint Goal Beat?	
Set 1						
Set 2						
Set 3						
Set 4						
Set 5						
Set 6						
re-done laps						
re-done laps						

Table 7. Sprint Day Log (Weeks 5 and 6)

Sprint Time Goal (carried over from Table 6)

Date		Sprint Goal Beat?		Sprint Goal Beat?		Sprint Goal Beat?	
Set 1							
Set 2							
Set 3							
Set 4							
Set 5							
Set 6							
Set 7							
re-done laps							
re-done laps							

Date		Sprint Goal Beat?		Sprint Goal Beat?		Sprint Goal Beat?	
Set 1							
Set 2							
Set 3							
Set 4							
Set 5							
Set 6							
Set 7							
re-done laps							
re-done laps							

Table 9. Sprint Day Log (Weeks 7 and 8)						
___ Sprint Time Goal (carried over from Table 8)						
Date	Sprint	Goal Beat?	Sprint	Goal Beat?	Sprint	Goal Beat?
Set 1						
Set 2						
Set 3						
Set 4						
Set 5						
Set 6						
Set 7						
Set 8						
re-done laps						
re-done laps						
Date	Sprint	Goal Beat?	Sprint	Goal Beat?	Sprint	Goal Beat?
Set 1						
Set 2						
Set 3						
Set 4						
Set 5						
Set 6						
Set 7						
Set 8						
re-done laps						
re-done laps						

Evaluation Logs

(Tables 4,6, 8, and 10)

Table 4. Evaluation Chart (Weeks 1 and 2)					
_____ Sum of set 1 from Table 3 (in seconds)	divided by _____ Number of times you completed set 1	X	0.9	____	A
_____ Sum of set 2 from Table 3 (in seconds)	divided by _____ Number of times you completed set 2	X	0.9	____	B
_____ Sum of set 3 from Table 3 (in seconds)	divided by _____ Number of times you completed set 3	X	0.9	____	C
_____ Sum of set 4 from Table 3 (in seconds)	divided by _____ Number of times you completed set 4	X	0.9	____	D
_____ Sum of set 5 from Table 3 (in seconds)	divided by _____ Number of times you completed set 5	X	0.9	____	E
A + B + C + D + E / 5	= _____				New Sprint Time Goal

Table 6. Evaluation Chart (Weeks 3 and 4)

_____ Sum of set 1 from Table 5 (in seconds)	divided by	_____ Number of times you completed set 1	X	0.9 ____ A
_____ Sum of set 2 from Table 5 (in seconds)	divided by	_____ Number of times you completed set 2	X	0.9 ____ B
_____ Sum of set 3 from Table 5 (in seconds)	divided by	_____ Number of times you completed set 3	X	0.9 ____ C
_____ Sum of set 4 from Table 5 (in seconds)	divided by	_____ Number of times you completed set 4	X	0.9 ____ D
_____ Sum of set 5 from Table 5 (in seconds)	divided by	_____ Number of times you completed set 5	X	0.9 ____ E
_____ Sum of set 6 from Table 5 (in seconds)	divided by	_____ Number of times you completed set 6	X	0.9 ____ F

A + B + C + D + E + F / 6   =   _____   New Sprint Time Goal

Table 8. Evaluation Chart (Weeks 5 and 6)						
_____	divided by	_____	X	0.9	_____	A
Sum of set 1 from Table 7 (in seconds)		Number of times you completed set 1				
_____	divided by	_____	X	0.9	_____	B
Sum of set 2 from Table 7 (in seconds)		Number of times you completed set 2				
_____	divided by	_____	X	0.9	_____	C
Sum of set 3 from Table 7 (in seconds)		Number of times you completed set 3				
_____	divided by	_____	X	0.9	_____	D
Sum of set 4 from Table 7 (in seconds)		Number of times you completed set 4				
_____	divided by	_____	X	0.9	_____	E
Sum of set 5 from Table 7 (in seconds)		Number of times you completed set 5				
_____	divided by	_____	X	0.9	_____	F
Sum of set 6 from Table 7 (in seconds)		Number of times you completed set 6				
_____	divided by	_____	X	0.9	_____	G
Sum of set 7 from Table 7 (in seconds)		Number of times you completed set 7				
A + B + C + D + E + F + G / 7			=	_____	New Sprint Time Goal	

Running Program
for Long Run Days

Table 11. Running Program for Long-Run Days	
Run for a minimum of:	
Week 1	20:00 minutes/day
Week 2	22:00 minutes/day
Week 3	24:00 minutes/day
Week 4	26:30 minutes/day
Week 5	28:30 minutes/day
Week 6	31:00 minutes/day
Week 7	33:30 minutes/day
Week 8	36:00 minutes/day

Push-up and Sit-up Evaluation Charts

(Tables 12 and 13)

Table 12. Push-up Evaluation Chart								
	Number of push-ups required to pass APFT							
Rest	2 minutes between sets							
Weeks 1-3 Duration		Day 1	Day 2	Day 3	Day 4	Day 5	Day 6	Day 7
Set 1	A* 1-minute							
	B* failure							
Set 2	A 1-minute							
	B failure							
Set 3	A 1-minute							
	B failure							
Rest	3 minutes between sets							
Weeks 4-6 Duration		Day 1	Day 2	Day 3	Day 4	Day 5	Day 6	Day 7
Set 1	A 1:30 minutes							
	B failure							
Set 2	A 1:30 minutes							
	B failure							
Set 3	A 1:30 minutes							
	B failure							
Rest	4 minutes between sets							
Weeks 7-8 Duration		Day 1	Day 2	Day 3	Day 4	Day 5	Day 6	Day 7
Set 1	A 2-minutes							
	B failure							
Set 2	A 2-minutes							
	B failure							
Set 3	A 2-minutes							
	B failure							
A*regular push-ups								
B*kneeling diamond push-ups								

Table 13. Sit-up Evaluation Chart								
	Number of sit-ups required to pass APFT							
Rest	2 minutes between sets							
Weeks 1-3 Duration		Day 1	Day 2	Day 3	Day 4	Day 5	Day 6	Day 7
Set 1 A* 1-minute								
B* failure								
Set 2 A 1-minute								
C* failure								
Rest	3 minutes between sets							
Weeks 4-6 Duration		Day 1	Day 2	Day 3	Day 4	Day 5	Day 6	Day 7
Set 1 A 1:30 minutes								
B failure								
Set 2 A 1:30 minutes								
C failure								
Rest	4 minutes between sets							
Weeks 7-8 Duration		Day 1	Day 2	Day 3	Day 4	Day 5	Day 6	Day 7
Set 1 A 2-minutes								
B failure								
Set 2 A 2-minutes								
C failure								
A*regular sit-ups								
B*abdominal crunches								
C*upper-half crunches								

Table 14. 8-Week Fitness Chart								
	Week 1	Week 2	Week 3	Week 4	Week 5	Week 6	Week 7	Week 8
Day 1	A	B	C (24 m)	B	D	B	C (33:30 m)	B
Day 2	B	D	B	C (26:30 m)	B	D	B	C (36 m)
Day 3	C (20 m)	B	D	B	C (28:30 m)	B	D	B
Day 4	B	C (22 m)	B	D	B	C (31 m)	B	D
Day 5	D	B	C (24 m)	B	D	B	C (33:30 m)	B
Day 6	B	D	B	C (26:30 m)	B	D	B	C (36 m)
Day 7	C (20 m)	B	D	B	C (28:30 m)	B (31 m)	D	B

A   1-mile assessment   m   minutes
B   push-ups and sit-ups
C   long run day
D   sprint day

Acronyms and Terms

Each branch of the military has its own terms and acronyms. In basic training, you will learn hundreds of acronyms, and you will be expected to know many of them by the time you arrive. Unfortunately, once you graduate basic training, there will be hundreds of acronyms and terms still to learn. Below is a list of acronyms and terms you will definitely hear at basic training. Marching commands are not included in this list. The more you study this list, the better off you will be at basic training.

Acronyms

AAFES: Army and Air Force Exchange Service
AAR: After Action Review
AGR: Active Guard Reserve
AIT: Advanced Individual Training
AMMO: Ammunition
ARNG: Army National Guard
APFT: Army Physical Fitness Test
ASAP: As Soon As Possible

ASVAB: Armed Forces Vocational Aptitude Battery

AT: Annual Training or Antitank

AWOL: Absent Without Leave

BAS: Basic Allowance for Subsistence

BC: Battalion Commander

BCG (RPG): Birth Control Glasses or Rape Prevention Glasses. Common acronyms associated with the standard issue military glasses.

BCT: Basic Combat Training

BDE: Brigade

BDU: Battle Dress Uniform

BHA: Basic Housing Allowance

BN: Battalion

BRM: Basic Rifle Marksmanship

CQ: Commanders Quarters or Charge of Quarters

CTMC: Community Troop Medical Clinic

D&C: Drill and Ceremony

DCU: Desert Camouflage Uniform

DFAC: Dining Facility. Also called Chow or Mess Hall.

DOB: Date of Birth

DOD: Department of Defense

DOR: Date of Rank

EEO: Equal Employment Opportunity

ELS: Entry Level Separation

EM: Enlisted Member

EN: Enlisted

EO: Equal Opportunity

EOCT: End of Cycle Training

FM: Field Manuals

FTX: Field Training Exercise

FYI: For Your Information

HMMWV: High mobility multipurpose-wheeled vehicle

IAW: In accordance with

ID: Infantry Division or Identification Card

IRR: Individual Ready Reserve

JAG: Judge Advocate General

KP: Kitchen Patrol

LBE: Load Bearing Equipment
LCE: Load Carrying Equipment
LES: Leave and Earnings Statement
MEPS: Military Entrance Processing Station
MI: Military Intelligence
MOPP: Mission Oriented Protective Posture
MOS: Military Occupational Specialty
MP: Military Police
MRE: Meal, Ready to Eat
NBC: Nuclear, Biological, Chemical
NCO: Noncommissioned Officer
NG: National Guard
NVG: Night Vision Goggles
OCS: Officer Candidate School
OSUT: One Station Unit Training
PG: Platoon Guide
PLDC: Primary Leadership Development Course.
PLT: Platoon
PMCS: Preventative Maintenance Checks and Services
PMOS: Primary Military Occupational Specialty
POV: Privately Owned Vehicle
POW: Prisoner of War
PT: Physical Training
PUP: Pick-up Point (usually seen on training schedules)
PX: Post Exchange
QM: Quartermaster
ROTC: Reserve Officer Training Corps
RSC: Regional Support Command
SAW: Squad Automatic Weapon
SGLI: Servicemen's Group Life Insurance
SOP: Standard Operating Procedure
SPORTS: Slap, Pull, Observe, Release, Tap, Squeeze (relating
    to BRM techniques)
SSN: Social Security Number
TIG: Time in Grade
TM: Technical Manual
TMC: Troop Medical Clinic

TRADOC: Training and Doctrine Command
UCMJ: Uniform Code of Military Justice
USAR: United States Army Reserve
USO: United Service Organization
UXO: Unexploded Ordnance
VA: Department of Veterans Affairs (formerly Veterans Administration)
VIP: Very Important Person
WO: Warrant Officer
XO: Executive Officer

Terms

550 cord: A commonly used rope practical for field use. Has a tensile strength of 550 pounds.
Article 15: A disciplinary statement commonly associated with the loss of rank or pay.
As you were: Disregard previous statement.
Ate up: Describes a soldier who can't do anything properly.
Battle rattle: Describes all equipment used to carry on ones person. In basic training, battle rattle usually consists of BDU's, flak vest, canteens, ammo pouches, magazine clips, Kevlar® helmet, weapon, pro-mask, rucksack, first-aid kit, and earplugs.
Beat your face: Perform push-ups.
Brass: A shell from a bullet.
Cadence: Songs performed while marching.
Chow hall: A military cafeteria.
Clip: See "magazine."
Class A Uniform: A military suit, displaying metals and ribbons, worn for special occasions.
Concertina wire: Circular barbed wire used to secure boundaries.
Contraband: Unauthorized material.
Convoy: A series of vehicles.
Cover: A hat.

Detail: A miscellaneous duty.

Dust your boots: Perform toe touches (see toe touches under miscellaneous exercises in chapter 2).

Fireguard: A duty which requires at least one soldier to guard an area or equipment while others are sleeping or performing other duties.

Flak: A protective vest worn during combat and training exercises.

Fraternization: Co-mingling with the opposite sex in an inappropriate manner.

Front Leaning Rest: See "beat your face."

Hazing: Tormenting another recruit by verbal or physical punishment.

High and tight: A common style of military haircut where the sides are shaved, or nearly shaved, with neatly trimmed hair remaining on the top.

Hospital Corner: A corner of a made-up bed in which the sheets have been neatly and securely folded. (See Chapter 12.)

Hot A: A hot meal provided to soldiers engaged in field work.

HUA (Hooah): A statement of acceptance which stands for I hear you, I understand you, and I acknowledge your statement (many meanings have derived from this acronym).

In cadence: A counting rhythm called while doing exercises.

Latrine: A bathroom.

Lima Charlie: Radio command meaning "I hear you loud and clear."

Magazine: A metal object used to hold bullets.

Mess Hall: See "Chow hall."

Over: Radio command signifying the end of a statement.

Out: Radio command signifying the end of a conversation.

Pass: Paperwork associated with allowing military personnel to leave an area for a specified duration of time.

Pogey: Bait Snacks

Prick: A handheld radio.

Profile: An order issued by a military doctor that prohibits performing a particular task or function.

Quartermaster: For basic training purposes only, quartermaster refers to a laundry submittal center.

Range: A field used to practice firing weapons.

Ranger Walk: To walk, heel to toe, at a fast pace.

Rappel Line: A rope that hangs from clothing to assist in rappelling.

Recycle: To be restarted and sent to a different basic training company.

Roger: Radio command meaning "ok."

Round: A bullet.

Rucksack: A backpack used to carry field gear.

Shakedown: A thorough inspection of certain items, an area, or personal belongings.

Sham Shield: A term associated with the specialist rank.

Smartbook: A book given to recruits during basic training which acts as a study guide and reference material.

Sincgar: A common radio in military vehicles.

Smoked: Punishment in the form of physical exercise. Also referred to as fluffing.

Snake: A shoelace sticking out of a boot.

Sound off: Speak louder.

Squared Away: Describes a soldier who has everything in order.

Stand Fast: Stay where you are until further notice.

TA-50: A series of field equipment inspected often by Drill Sergeants.

Toes on line: A fingernail and toenail inspection performed by Drill Sergeants before bedtime.

Top: Another name for a first sergeant. (Do not call your first sergeant this name in basic training).

INDEX

Notes

Use these pages to record your thoughts, observations, and personal suggestions.

About the Author: Sergeant Michael Volkin is a U.S. Army veteran. He served in Operation Enduring/Iraqi Freedom as a Chemical Operations Specialist, and received an Army Commendation Medal for his efforts and for the fitness programs he designed to help his fellow soldiers. Michael has a Bachelor's and Master's degree in Science from Stephen F. Austin State University in Texas. He lives and works in northern California.